Growth Mindset Workbook for Kids

GROWTH MINDSET

WORKBOOK for KIDS

55 Fun Activities to Think Creatively, Solve Problems, and Love Learning

PEYTON CURLEY

ILLUSTRATED BY TYLER PARKER

ROCKRIDGE PRESS

**To the West End School (Louisville, Kentucky)
Class of 2025, for being the fuel for my passion.
YOU CAN BE ANYTHING YOU DREAM OF.**

Interior and Cover Designer: Lisa Forde
Art Producer: Janice Ackerman
Editor: Samantha Barbaro
Production Manager: Holly Haydash
Production Editor: Sigi Nacson

Illustrations © Tyler Parker, 2020

ISBN: Print 978-1-64611-703-1
Ebook 978-1-64611-704-8
R1

Contents

A Letter to Grown-ups **viii**

A Letter to Kids **xi**

CHAPTER 1
What Does "Growth Mindset" Mean? 1

Mindset Quiz **4**

Which Kind of Mindset Is This? **8**

CHAPTER 2
Look at All These Awesome Mistakes! 17

That "Oops" Feeling **20**

Drawing in the Dark **20**

All Shapes and Sizes **24**

What Went Wrong? **26**

Accepting Responsibility **27**

You're the Expert **31**

Flip the Slip **32**

My Mistake Plan **33**

If I Never Made a Mistake . . . **35**

Say What? **35**

Dear Mistake **37**

Positive Affirmations **40**

Keep On Rolling **41**

$7 \times 6 = 42$

$7 \times 7 = 49$

$7 \times 8 = 56$

$7 \times 9 = 63$

CHAPTER 3
Be an Amazing Problem Solver! 43

My Problem Plan 46
More Than One Solution 47
Advice for a Friend 48
Feedback Mindset 51
Think, Restate, Thank, Decide 52
Better Today 54
Look How I've Grown! 54
A-*Maze*-ing Improvement 55
What Challenges Me? 58
Just Like the Movies 59
Learning to Love It 60
Things I Can't Do . . . Yet 63
Use What You've Got 64
You're Right! 65

CHAPTER 4
Get Creative and Keep Trying! 67

Draw Outside the Box 70
This Used to Be a . . . 71
Silly Solutions 72
Let's Do It Again . . . and Again! 75
To My Friend Who Doesn't Practice 76
Think Before You Plan 79
Break It Down 80
More Than a Band-Aid 82
Saying Is Believing 85
What If They Had Given Up? 86

CHAPTER 5
Set Goals, and Then Set More Goals! 89

A World Without Goals 92
Wheel of Fortune 92
I Can See It Now . . . 94
My Goal Selfie 95
Knowledge Is Power 98
Step by Step 99
That's Backward! 100
Mirror, Mirror on the Wall 103
Move Your Goalpost 104
Dream Bigger! 105

CHAPTER 6
Keep Going! 107

Dear Me: Don't Give Up! 110
Here's Why I Am Awesome 111
Stretch Your Mindset 114
My Mantra 116
Who Can Help? 119
Check Out My Questions 120
Fill My Brain 123
3, 2, Wonder 124
Look How Far You've Come! 125

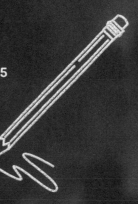

Glossary 130
Resources for Kids 132
Resources for Grown-ups 133
Index 135

A Letter to GROWN-UPS

Whether you are a parent, guardian, teacher, counselor, or other mentor, I'd like to thank you for your commitment to furthering the social emotional development of a child. As a former elementary school teacher, I have seen the power that a growth mindset can have in a student's life. I've seen children who were so hesitant to make mistakes that they avoided work become self-motivated, confident, and high-achieving students after learning and applying a growth mindset.

Without the right tools and strategies, many children get stuck in a fixed mindset. A fixed mindset is the belief that our abilities, talents, and intelligence are static: We are either good at something or we aren't. This way of thinking is limiting and holds children (and adults) back from reaching their full potential. A growth mindset is the belief that our abilities, talents, and intelligence can grow or change through effort and perseverance. A growth mindset equips children with the skills to work through challenges, set and achieve goals, and think creatively. It boosts self-esteem and encourages educational risks.

This book teaches kids the difference between a fixed mindset and a growth mindset in an engaging way. They will learn the actual brain science behind why a growth mindset works. The exercises in this book are designed to cultivate a growth mindset in children. They address such concepts as learning from mistakes, problem solving through multiple approaches, using feedback, goal setting, positive thinking, and more. The shift from a fixed to a growth mindset isn't easy. It involves risk taking and requires children to try and fail and try again.

Here are some tips for how you can support children through this process:

- Use and encourage language that reflects your own growth mindset. For example, instead of saying, "I can't do it" to your child, try saying, "I'm still working on improving."

- Accept mistakes as learning opportunities. Share examples of your own mistakes and discuss how you were able to learn and grow as a result.

- Help children regulate emotions. There are a lot of uncomfortable emotions associated with trying new things, making mistakes, and failing. Some simple strategies for regulating these emotions include taking deep breaths, counting to ten and back, going for a short walk, and drinking a glass of water.

- Give praise for effort, creativity, and problem solving. Recognize growth, rather than just achievement.

- Encourage curiosity.

- Familiarize yourself with the brain science behind a growth mindset (covered in chapter 1), and remind children as they struggle that their brain is growing and changing.

Encourage your child to get started on the exercises. Offer support along the way, and be excited! If you are, they will be, too!

A Letter to KIDS

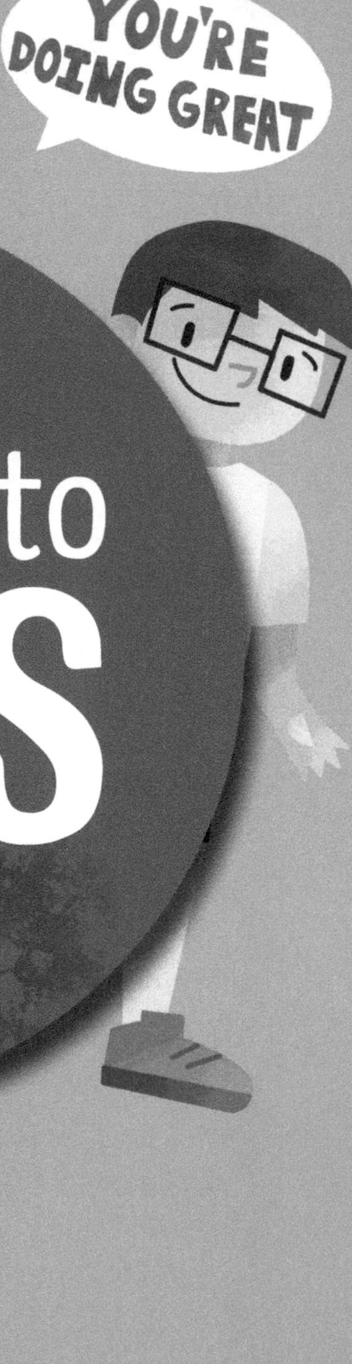

Have you ever thought, "Maybe I'm just not a math person" or "Some people just aren't good at art, and I'm one of them"? What if I told you that just by changing the way you think, you could become a "math person" or improve your skills in art? What if I told you that you could become a better reader or soccer player or actor, or, well, *anything you want*? Well, you can! You just need a **growth mindset**. With a growth mindset, you can actually change your brain! A growth mindset is the belief that how smart you are and how good you are at something can actually *change* with hard work. That means that as long as you are willing to work through challenges and keep going when things get tough, you can achieve pretty much anything you want! With a growth mindset, the possibilities are endless.

In this book, you will learn more about what a growth mindset is, why it's important, and how your brain changes when you have one. You'll get to try fun exercises and activities that will help you practice having a growth mindset, so you can go out in the world and be AMAZING!

All the fun exercises in this book were made *just for you*. They work best if you go in order, but if you get stuck on one, it's okay to move ahead and go back later. After all, a growth mindset is all about pushing forward when things get tough. Nothing should get in the way of becoming a growth mindset expert!

It's time for chapter 1, where you'll learn all about what a growth mindset really is and how it can help you achieve *amazing* things. Repeat after me: "I CAN DO AMAZING THINGS!" Good job. Now you're all ready for chapter 1!

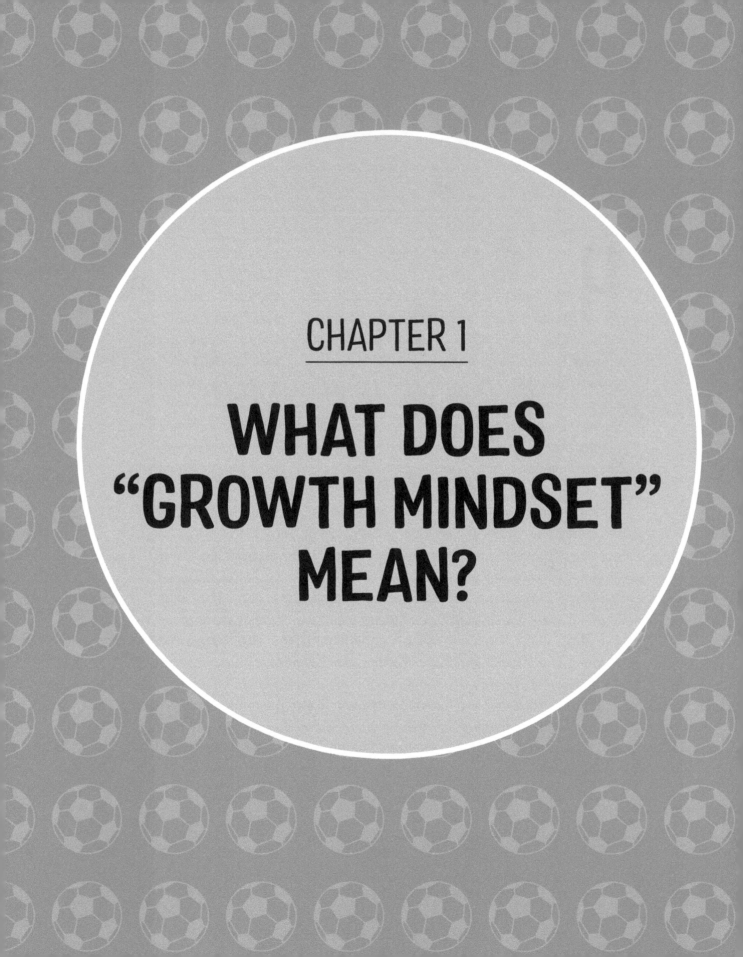

CHAPTER 1

WHAT DOES "GROWTH MINDSET" MEAN?

Your brain is a lot like the muscles in your body. When you use a muscle over and over again, it gets stronger. The same is true of your brain! You can actually train your brain to get smarter. This is a big part of the growth mindset. When you have a growth mindset, you understand that practicing a skill or studying information can grow and change your brain. A growth mindset is believing that you can learn new things and improve your skills with practice. People who have a growth mindset are more likely to be successful because they push themselves to keep learning and growing. When someone has a **fixed mindset**, they don't believe they can get better at something through practice. People with a fixed mindset often give up instead of working harder. In this chapter, you will learn all about the growth mindset and begin to discover how it can help you achieve amazing things in your life.

So, what is a fixed mindset?

"I didn't make the basketball team last year, so I guess I'm not good enough to make it this year, either."

"I never get good grades on my math tests, so there's no point in studying."

"What's the point of going to art class? I'll never be good at drawing."

These kids all have a fixed mindset. They believe that all their skills and abilities are "fixed," meaning they can't change. They don't believe that hard work and practice can change how good or bad they are at something. Once a person with a fixed mindset decides they aren't good at something, they just quit trying. Having a fixed mindset will hold you back from trying new things or becoming the best you can be at something. If you are feeling like you've had a fixed mindset in the past, don't worry! We are going to work toward changing that through the activities in this book.

What is a growth mindset?

"I didn't make the basketball team last year, but I have been practicing every day to try again."

"I have been struggling in math, but I know if I keep studying and work with my teacher, I can improve my grades."

"I'm not the best artist in the class, but I'm getting better with practice."

These kids all have a growth mindset. They believe that their skills and abilities can change or grow with practice. They don't give up when they are facing a challenge. When someone has a growth mindset, they are more open to trying new things because they aren't afraid of failing. Having this mindset gives people more opportunities in life. A growth mindset doesn't make it easier to learn new things or improve your skills. You will still have to work hard, but when someone has a growth mindset, they know that putting in the extra effort will be worth it.

Mindset Quiz

The first step to having a growth mindset is understanding your thinking! Not sure which mindset you have? You can take this quiz to see which mindset you mostly have right now. Be sure to answer each question honestly. To have a growth mindset, we have to be honest with ourselves, even when it is hard.

EVENT	I'D SAY . . .	OR I'D SAY . . .
You failed this week's vocabulary quiz.	I guess I'm just not good at remembering definitions.	Next time I'll practice and study harder. I bet I could get all of them right.
You didn't make the soccer team.	I'll never be good enough to make the team.	I bet I could make the soccer team next year if I practice more.
You got in trouble for talking during class.	I'm always going to get in trouble at school because I have trouble being quiet.	I can work on my self-control and improve my behavior.
You didn't get a part in the school play.	I guess I'm just not that good at acting.	I'll talk to the drama teacher and ask how I can improve for the next play.
You hurt a friend's feelings when you lost your temper.	It's not my fault that I have a temper. I can't help it.	I'll apologize to my friend. Next time, I'll take deep breaths to calm down instead of losing my temper.
You left your homework sitting on the kitchen table.	I just have a bad memory, so I forget things a lot.	Next time, I'll put it in my backpack before bed so I don't forget.
You missed the game-winning shot in your basketball game.	I'm not good at basketball. I guess I should quit the team.	I'll keep practicing my shooting. Maybe I'll make the next one.
You got a D on your math test this week.	I'm just not a good math student.	I'll get a tutor for some extra help in math.
You rushed through your project and got a bad grade.	I'm too busy for school projects. I always get bad grades.	Next time, I'll take my time on the project instead of waiting until the night before.
You keep messing up one part of the song you are supposed to play at your piano recital.	This song is just too hard for me, no matter how much I practice.	I'll practice the tricky part with my piano teacher before the recital.

How many yellow answers did you choose? This will be your fixed mindset score. _____ /10

How many blue answers did you choose? This will be your growth mindset score. _____ /10

If you chose more blue answers, you probably lean toward a growth mindset. If you chose more yellow answers, you might be reacting to situations with a fixed mindset.

Go back and look at each blue answer. Notice how the blue answers show that you aren't giving up and that you believe you can improve. This kind of thinking is helpful and shows a growth mindset! Even if you are already leaning toward a growth mindset, you can use the exercises in this workbook to improve your mindset even more!

Now read the yellow answers and think about how those responses could hold you back from learning and growing. This kind of thinking is *not* helpful. If you chose more yellow answers, or if you've said things like that in the past, don't worry. You have already taken a step toward a growth mindset by taking time to reflect on your own thinking. This workbook can help you take even more steps toward a growth mindset. Practice makes permanent. The more you practice having a growth mindset, the more permanent this way of thinking will become.

That sounds great! How can I have a growth mindset?

You've learned what it looks like to have a growth mindset or a fixed mindset, but most people really have a little bit of both. Think of it like a scale from 0 to 10, with 0 being someone who has a fixed mindset *all the time* and 10 being someone who has a growth mindset *all the time*. Someone who is a 5 would have a fixed mindset half of the time and a growth mindset the other half of the time. The good thing about mindset being on a scale is that your spot on the scale can shift. Once you know the secret of what a growth mindset can do, which you are learning through the activities in this book, you can get *your* mindset number closer to a 10. If you aren't sure where to start, try some of these tips for having a growth mindset:

- When something is challenging, try a new strategy.
- Think of challenges as new chances for you to learn and grow.
- Instead of using the word "failing," try using the word "learning."
- Focus on the progress you are making instead of how much further you have to go.
- Reward yourself for hard work.
- Ask for help when you need it.
- When you make a mistake, take time to think about how it can help you in the future.

Another helpful tip for developing your growth mindset is to give your-self a little encouragement. The way we speak to ourselves affects the way we feel, act, and think. When you are feeling frustrated or chal-lenged, avoid saying things like "I can't do it!" or "I give up!" Instead, try saying something from this list:

- I haven't met my **goal** *yet*, but I am working hard.
- I can do hard things with hard work.
- I learn from my **mistakes**.
- I get better every time I practice.
- I am on the right track.
- I help my brain grow by learning hard things.
- I don't give up.
- I can try another way.
- I am proud of myself for trying.

Which Kind of Mindset Is This?

Read each of the statements and decide if it shows a fixed mindset or a growth mindset. Circle your answer.

I haven't figured it out . . . yet.	fixed	growth
I just can't do this.	fixed	growth
I'm not good at this.	fixed	growth
I'll keep practicing.	fixed	growth
It's so hard, but I won't give up.	fixed	growth
I'll never be good enough.	fixed	growth
I will ask for help.	fixed	growth
I'm either good or I'm not.	fixed	growth
I can improve through hard work.	fixed	growth
No one can help me.	fixed	growth

ANSWER KEY

I haven't figured it out . . . yet.	growth
I just can't do this.	fixed
I'm not good at this.	fixed
I'll keep practicing.	growth
It's so hard, but I won't give up.	growth
I'll never be good enough.	fixed
I will ask for help.	growth
I'm either good or I'm not.	fixed
I can improve through hard work.	growth
No one can help me.	fixed

Wow, look at you GROW! You're already getting the hang of this whole mindset thing. The more you focus on a growth mindset, the easier it will be to have a growth mindset yourself. You can pay attention to how your friends, families, and teachers think. You can even notice the mindset of the characters in your favorite movies, TV shows, and books. Celebrities can have a growth mindset, too!

Now that you've become an expert in identifying both types of mindsets, it's time to learn a little bit more about your brain and how having a growth mindset affects it. After that, you'll be ready to jump right into some exercises. These will help you practice a growth mindset and achieve your goals!

Your awesome brain can do so much!

Your brain is capable of incredible things. Every time you learn something, try something new, work through a problem, or practice a skill, your brain is changing and growing. You see, your brain has these tiny cells called **neurons**, which help us think, feel, and act.

When you struggle with something, your neurons struggle, too. But this struggle is actually a good thing! When neurons struggle, they look to other neurons for support, just the way you might ask a friend or family member for help when you are having a hard time with something. While you are working hard at learning, your neurons are making connections with each other. These connections let your brain work faster and smarter. The harder a challenge is, the more your neurons can grow. Think of your brain like a muscle. When you use a muscle in your body over and over again, what happens? It gets stronger, of course! Your brain works the same way. The more you use it, the stronger it gets.

All this science can seem a little confusing at first, but guess what? Reading and thinking about new information is one way to make those awesome new connections between neurons in your brain. That means your brain is actually changing *right now*!

Because we understand how the brain works, we know that our ability to do different things is not fixed. Our abilities can change as our brains change and make new connections. This is why having a fixed mindset limits us from doing all the amazing things we are capable of. If we believe that our brains can't change or grow, then we will never try new and challenging things. Without new and challenging experiences, our brains stay fixed. That's why a growth mindset is so powerful. When we believe in the power of our brain, we work through challenges because we know that each challenge is making our brain stronger and smarter. If you keep practicing or working at a challenge, it will eventually become another ability or strength that you have. Trying new things and working through challenges isn't easy, but if you keep it up, your brain will thank you!

Be kind to your brain!

We know that our brains can change and grow, so why does it feel like it's taking *forever* sometimes? Hang in there. It takes a little patience to allow our brains to do their job. Just the way it takes time for your body to grow, your brain needs time, too. Trying something one time probably isn't enough to change it from a challenge to an ability—this takes repeated practice and hard work. You might not notice the changes right away, but if you stick with it, you'll see that the challenge starts to get easier. Feeling that something is difficult is actually good news for your brain. If it doesn't feel hard, your brain probably isn't changing!

When you do new or hard things, it's important to be kind to your brain. Your brain is learning along with you! Imagine you were working on a tricky math problem and someone said, "You'll never get it! You're not smart enough!" How would you feel? Well, just like we want others to be kind and encouraging to us when we try to new things, we should be kind and encouraging to ourselves. The way you talk to your brain can affect your mindset, your patience, and your **perseverance**. Talk to your brain the way you would talk to a friend. After all, your brain *is* your friend!

TIPS FOR TALKING TO YOUR BRAIN

|||||||||||||||||||||||||||||||||||||||||||||||||||||||||||||||||||||||||||||||||||

1. **Give your brain compliments.** Thinking positive thoughts about yourself helps strengthen your growth mindset.

2. **Forgive yourself (and your brain) for mistakes.** Remember, **mistakes** help us grow!

3. **Practice gratitude.** Thank your brain for all the hard work it is doing to help you learn a new skill.

4. **Be a cheerleader for your brain.** Say encouraging things to your brain, like "You can do it!" or "You've got this!"

If the science of your brain isn't enough to convince you of the power of a mindset, here are some examples of a growth mindset in action.

Growth mindset in action

Jackson really wanted to be able to read as well as the other fourth graders in his class, but he just couldn't seem to keep up. He was very hardworking, but he had dyslexia, which made processing letters harder for him than for most of his classmates. Some days he felt like he would never be good enough, but one day, he decided to ask for help. He talked to his mom about his struggles and set up a meeting with his teacher. The three of them came up with a plan for Jackson to practice at home and to work with a tutor two days a week after school. Jackson knew it wouldn't be easy, but he put in the work that they'd agreed on. By the end of the school year, Jackson could read the same books his friends were reading.

Football tryouts at school were coming up, and Kennedy had always dreamed of being a football player. The only problem was that her school only had a team for boys. She didn't think this was fair, since she loved playing football and worked just as hard as the boys on the team. She wasn't going to let this stop her. Kennedy went to the principal and asked if she could be allowed to try out for the team. The principal decided to give her a chance. She practiced every day after school for the three weeks leading up to tryouts. She ignored the boys who teased her and said girls couldn't play football. When tryouts finally rolled around, Kennedy made the team!

Grace has always loved science, so she was really excited when she learned that her school was hosting a science fair. She couldn't wait to enter, but when she saw other students starting to bring in their projects, she got worried. "Wow," she thought, "everyone must have gotten help at home. My mom works two jobs, and she doesn't have time to help me. She can't afford all the fancy supplies my classmates used." She began to feel discouraged, but instead of giving up, Grace decided to work through the challenge. She knew she was great at science and could do a great job without fancy supplies or help. On the day of the science fair, Grace proudly presented her project. Her classmates were all impressed, and she earned the first-place prize.

Jayden saw his classmates getting rewarded for staying on task and completing their work on time. He felt disappointed because he never earned the same rewards. Jayden's doctor told him he had something called ADHD, which made it harder for him to sit still and concentrate for as long as other kids in his class. He told his teacher he just couldn't do it because of his ADHD. His teacher talked to him about having a growth mindset and working through challenges. He set up a plan with his teacher that allowed him to take short breaks every thirty minutes to get his brain refocused. As long as he got right back to work afterward, his teacher would allow him to keep taking the breaks. The next week, he earned the reward for staying on task!

Nia tried out for the competitive soccer team last year, but she didn't make it. She felt angry and embarrassed about not making the team and wanted to quit soccer forever. Nia's dad told her a story about how he didn't make the basketball team during his first year of high school and then came back the next year to be the lead scorer. He said just because she didn't make it this year didn't mean she couldn't get better. Nia decided to talk to the coach and ask what she needed to improve on. She worked with her dad for a whole year, practicing the soccer drills the coach had suggested. When she tried out for the team again this year, she made it! She even scored two goals in her first game of the season.

You've learned all about growth mindset and how the brain works, so now it's time to put your brain to the test! Get ready for some fun, exciting, and creative exercises to strengthen your growth mindset. In chapter 2, you will discover how amazing mistakes are. Hey, I know what you're thinking. *Amazing mistakes? Mistakes can't be amazing!* Well, chapter 2 just might change your mind.

LOOK AT ALL THESE AWESOME MISTAKES!

Did someone say *mistakes*? That's right! Maybe you've thought that mistakes are bad, or are embarrassing, or mean you're a failure. They can make us feel pretty lousy, but we can change that by changing our mindset, or how we think about mistakes. Mistakes aren't meant to be avoided or forgotten. Mistakes are an important part of learning and growing. In fact, your brain actually changes and grows more when you make a mistake than when you get it right on the first try. Our brains make new connections every time we make a mistake and fix it. These new connections make us smarter! Changing the way you think about and respond to mistakes will give you the most opportunity for success. Still not excited about mistakes? After you complete the exercises in this chapter, you will see just how awesome mistakes really are.

How you feel after mistakes

"I am so stupid for missing that math problem."

"I really messed up on my last art project, so I guess I'm just not good at art."

"I feel like I'm a bad kid because I got in trouble for talking during a test."

We have all made mistakes, and we have all felt bad about them. Uncomfortable emotions, such as sadness, anger, disappointment, and embarrassment, are common after making a mistake. Sometimes when a person makes mistakes, they feel like a failure and want to give up. They believe they'll never be good enough to get it right.

A growth mindset has a different take on mistakes. It's still normal to feel disappointed or embarrassed when you mess up, but having a growth mindset means being able to move past these emotions. Instead of staying stuck in those feelings, you can shift your emotions by changing the way you respond to the mistake. When someone has a growth mindset, they see a mistake as an opportunity to learn and grow. They are able to manage their emotions in a way that helps them achieve more.

Think about the first example at the start of this section, where a student feels bad after missing a math problem. Have you ever missed a math problem? How did that make *you* feel? Missing a math problem is really no big deal, but it can feel pretty big when the whole class is watching you or when your grade on a test depends on getting it right. What happens if you just say, "I am so stupid" and keep feeling bad about yourself? How will you do on the next math test? Deciding you'll never be good enough to get it right is an example of a fixed mindset. Instead, you can practice a growth mindset. You can choose to let your mistake help you. That's right, *you* can *choose*! How you respond to your mistakes is up to you, and it can make a big difference in how you achieve your goals. It's important to be able to manage the uncomfortable emotions that come with making mistakes before we can use the mistakes to help us. Take a look at these strategies for handling the big emotions that come with making a mistake.

STEPS FOR MANAGING EMOTIONS WHEN YOU MAKE A MISTAKE:

1. Notice how you feel. Are you embarrassed? Worried about getting in trouble? Angry? These feelings are normal. Allow yourself to feel the emotion.

2. Take three deep breaths and focus on letting that emotion go.

3. Reflect on your mistake. What caused it? What could you have done differently?

4. Decide how you want to use your mistake to help you. Focus on how you'll feel when you have achieved this outcome.

In the next section, we'll learn a little more about steps 3 and 4, but first, let's practice noticing how mistakes make us feel.

That "Oops" Feeling

We've all felt that "oops" feeling. Think about a mistake you have made. Write about how you felt afterward.

Mistakes don't always feel good, but don't worry! The exercises in this book will help you change the way you feel about making mistakes.

Drawing in the Dark

In this exercise, you will be drawing a picture in the dark. You will need a pencil for this activity.

BEFORE

Predict: What thoughts or concerns do you have about drawing a picture in the dark? How do you think it will feel to draw a picture without being able to see?

TIME TO DRAW

Turn off the lights, close your eyes, and draw a picture of a boat sailing across the ocean. Do your very best work, and keep your eyes closed the whole time you draw!

AFTERWARD

Open your eyes and look at your picture. What mistakes did you make?

Reflect: How did you feel while you were drawing the picture? How did you feel when you opened your eyes and looked at it?

Sometimes worrying about making a mistake feels worse than actually making the mistake. You might have felt frustrated or anxious while you were drawing. But guess what? You tried your best, and that is something to be proud of. Maybe you don't feel satisfied with the work you did, but that's what erasers are for! Now you can go back and fix the mistakes in your drawing. Notice how you feel while you make the changes.

But mistakes can be good!

Mistakes may not feel good at first, but they are a great opportunity for you to become even more awesome. When you make a mistake, you have the chance to think about what went wrong and what you can do better next time. Without taking that time to reflect, your mistake won't help you.

Imagine you miss a question on a test. Think about what happened that caused you to miss that question. Did you study hard enough? Are you still confused about the material? Were you just rushing? Think about what you could have done differently. **Reflecting** on, or thinking about, your mistakes helps keep you from making the same mistake over and over. Instead of feeling discouraged, you can choose to feel motivated to do better next time.

When you make a mistake, you need to think about what kind of mistake it was. Mistakes come in all shapes and sizes. There are big mistakes, like cheating on a test, and there are small mistakes, like forgetting your umbrella on a rainy day. Big mistakes usually have big consequences, and small mistakes usually have small consequences. A **consequence** is something that happens as a result of a decision or an action.

Let's think about what the consequence would be for your small mistake. If you forget your umbrella on a rainy day, you will probably get wet. This is a small consequence that has a small effect on your day. Now think about the possible consequences for your big mistake: cheating on a test. You might have to go to the principal's office. You might get a zero on the test, which will bring your whole grade down. Big mistakes have big consequences. When you make a mistake, ask yourself, "What was the size of my mistake? What was the consequence of my mistake?" Knowing these things can help you decide how to improve in the future.

It's also important to think about whom your mistake affects. Some mistakes only affect you, but other mistakes affect other people, too. For example, if you forget to wear your jacket on a cold day, *you* will feel cold, but it's likely no one else will be affected by this mistake. If you forget to do your part in a group project, you *and* your whole group will be affected. The whole group might get a lower grade because you didn't do your part. It is important to consider how your actions affect other people. In the next exercise, you will practice deciding the size of mistakes and whom they affect.

Next Time . . .

I didn't study and rushed through my math test. The score wasn't so good. I know I could have done better. I'll use this mistake to help me. Next time I'll study and take more time with the questions.

All Shapes and Sizes

Take a look at each of these mistakes and decide: Is it a big mistake or a small mistake? Will it affect only me, or will others be affected, too?

Here's an example:

I was jealous of my friend so I spread a rumor about her.

 **Big mistake**   **Small mistake**

Only affects me   **Affects other people**

Now you try:

I left my lunch at home so my mom had to leave work to bring it to me.

Big mistake   **Small mistake**

Only affects me   **Affects other people**

I decided to play outside with my friends instead of studying for my test.

Big mistake   **Small mistake**

Only affects me   **Affects other people**

I left my homework sitting on the counter this morning.

Big mistake   **Small mistake**

Only affects me   **Affects other people**

I lost my temper and pushed my classmate at recess because he was teasing me.

Big mistake   **Small mistake**

Only affects me   **Affects other people**

I skipped soccer practice so I didn't get to play in the game with my team on Saturday.

Big mistake   **Small mistake**

Only affects me   **Affects other people**

I was making jokes and distracting other students while the teacher was talking.

Big mistake   **Small mistake**

Only affects me   **Affects other people**

I forgot to wear my gym shoes and I have PE today.

Big mistake   **Small mistake**

Only affects me   **Affects other people**

I ran out of time to finish my homework before class so I copied my friend's paper.

Big mistake   **Small mistake**

Only affects me   **Affects other people**

What Went Wrong?

It's important to be able to think about our mistakes and decide what went wrong, or what caused the mistake and how we could fix it or keep it from happening again. Think about a mistake you have made before. Fill in the diagram below.

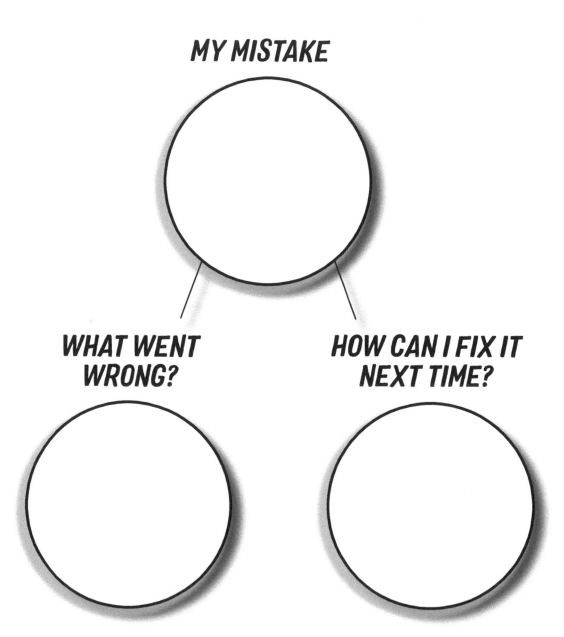

MY MISTAKE

WHAT WENT WRONG?

HOW CAN I FIX IT NEXT TIME?

Accepting Responsibility

Accepting responsibility for our choices helps us grow. We can't learn from our mistakes if we just blame them on other people or situations.

Instead of saying things like:

"I didn't do it! He's lying!"

"I only did it because she told me to."

"If they hadn't made me mad, I wouldn't have done it!"

"It wasn't my fault."

You should:

1. Own your mistakes. Be honest and say what you did wrong.

2. Reflect on your mistake. Why did you do it? Avoid blaming others or making excuses.

3. Repair any harm that was done because of the mistake. Did you hurt anyone's feelings or inconvenience anyone? Do you owe someone an apology?

4. Use this information to make better choices in the future.

Think of a mistake you have made in the past, and practice accepting responsibility by filling in the blanks.

I accept responsibility for _____.

I made that choice because _____.

I need to repair it by _____.

I can make better choices in the future by _____.

Mistakes are awesome learning opportunities

You have learned how to recognize and manage the emotions that come with making mistakes. You have also practiced identifying and taking responsibility for your mistakes. Now you're ready for the really awesome part! You can learn from your mistakes! Mistakes are one of the best ways we can learn. Remember how we learned all about those neurons in the brain? They work hardest when we make mistakes, and when they are working hard, our brain is growing and changing.

Learning from your mistakes does take a little work, but trust me, it's worth it. Taking time to learn from mistakes keeps us from making the same mistakes over and over again. It also makes us smarter and more capable of achieving our goals. There are a few types of learning opportunities that can happen when we make a mistake. Knowing which type of learning opportunity your mistake is can help you decide what to do next.

Accidental success. Sometimes we make a mistake that ends up working out. We can use this to change our ideas of what works and what doesn't.

This opportunity might look like:

- You're working on a science experiment and you accidentally use the wrong material, but the experiment ends up working better.
- You're working on an art project and you accidentally mix the wrong colors for your paint, but the color ends up looking exactly how you had imagined!

One step closer. This type of learning opportunity happens when we're stretching past what we can already do without help. You can use the knowledge you already have, but you're likely to make mistakes as you expand your skills. These mistakes can help you grow toward your goal.

This opportunity might look like:

- You are reading out loud from a book that is just a little above your reading level and you mispronounce a few words.
- You're already an expert in multiplying 1-digit numbers by 2-digit numbers, but you're trying to multiply 2-digit numbers by 2-digit numbers and you miss a few of the problems.

I knew better. This type of learning opportunity happens when we make a mistake that could have been avoided. It's a sloppy mistake or something we knew we shouldn't have done. These learning opportunities can remind us to try our best and make smarter choices.

This opportunity might look like:

- You rush through a test.
- You accidentally circle an incorrect answer and don't check your work before turning it in.

Never again. There are some mistakes that have very big conse-quences. They may be dangerous or cause serious harm. These are the learning opportunities that should teach us to *never* make that mistake again.

This opportunity might look like:

- You didn't look both ways before crossing a street, and a car almost hit you.
- You ran away from home when your parents made you angry.

Here are some questions you can ask yourself when you make a mistake:

- What was my mistake?
- Why did I make this mistake?
- Which type of learning opportunity is it?
- What can I do to prevent this mistake from happening again?
- What do I need to do to make it right?

Next Time . . .

Mrs. Thompson said we could go to recess once we finished our science test. I really wanted to play on the computer for recess. I knew if I wanted a turn on the computer, I had to finish my test first. I rushed through the test and turned it in. When I got my test back, it was a D-. I knew rushing through the test wasn't the right choice. Next time, I'll remember that my test is more important than recess and take my time.

You're the Expert

Think about a mistake you have made in the past. Which type of learning opportunity was it? Imagine you are giving advice to a friend who made this mistake. What would you tell them?

Flip the Slip

Sometimes mistakes are called "slips" or "slipups." Read each mistake and think of a way you can "flip the slip" into a learning opportunity.

You skipped your afternoon math tutoring because you wanted to play basketball with your friends instead. That night, you couldn't do any of the problems in your homework.	
You promised your friend Cara you would help her study for the vocabulary quiz tomorrow, but you bailed on her when Alexa invited you to hang out at her house. Now Cara is upset with you.	
You didn't feel like practicing piano this week. When you got to your recital rehearsal, you were embarrassed because you messed up the tricky part of the song.	
You told your parents you would clean your room before you played video games. You really wanted to play video games, so you shoved everything under your bed. Your mom checked under your bed. You lost your video game privileges for a week.	
You forgot you had a spelling test today, so you didn't study. You peeked over at your classmate's paper during the test to see her answers. Your teacher caught you.	

My Mistake Plan

Think of a mistake you made recently. Choose three strategies from this list that you want to try and place a check in the box. Any time you make a mistake or get stuck, you can come back to this list to make a plan.

When I make a mistake, I can . . .

- ❑ Take deep breaths to manage my emotions.
- ❑ Forgive myself.
- ❑ Remind myself that I am allowed to make mistakes.
- ❑ Apologize if I hurt someone.
- ❑ Take actions to make it right.
- ❑ Identify which type of learning opportunity it is.
- ❑ Brainstorm ways to do it better next time.
- ❑ Remind myself that I am one step closer to getting it right.
- ❑ Talk to someone about how I am feeling.
- ❑ Ask for help.
- ❑ Try again.

Sometimes mistakes are just awesome

Did you know that some pretty amazing inventions were made completely by mistake? If you still aren't convinced of how awesome mistakes can be, check out these stories about regular people whose mistakes led to new inventions used by people all over the world.

Have you ever played with Silly Putty? Many kids love playing with the bouncy, stretchy, slimy putty, but it was actually invented by complete accident! James Wright was an engineer at General Electric during World War II. He was attempting to invent a special type of rubber substitute to be used for airplane tires, soldiers' boots, and other equipment for the war. He added boric acid to a silicone oil substance he was testing, and ended up with a gooey, bouncy mess! It didn't work for airplane tires, but kids around the world have enjoyed Silly Putty ever since!

Do you love chocolate chip cookies? Ruth Wakefield, the creator of the chocolate chip cookie, actually made it by accident. She was trying to make chocolate cookies, when she realized she was out of baking chocolate. She decided to break a piece of semisweet chocolate into small pieces and mix them in with the dough. She expected the chocolate to melt and mix together with the dough, but instead she ended up with the first batch of chocolate chip cookies.

James Wright and Ruth Wakefield were able to come up with new inventions because they weren't afraid to fail. They tried new things and experimented. They paid attention to what worked and what didn't. They learned from what didn't work and also got a bit lucky. Think about what the world would be like without Silly Putty and chocolate chip cookies! And these are only two of many inventions that were created by mistake. Some other awesome mistakes include Play-Doh, artificial sweetener, Post-it notes, and X-rays!

If I Never Made a Mistake . . .

Write about what your life would be like if you never made a mistake. Reflect on all the valuable lessons you have learned from mistakes along the way, and what your life would be like if you hadn't learned from them.

Say What?

"I was born to make mistakes, not to fake perfection."
—Drake, rapper

What does this quote mean to you?

"Many of life's failures are people who did not realize how close they were to success when they gave up."
—Thomas Edison, inventor

What does this quote mean to you?

"I always say the minute I stop making mistakes is the minute I stop learning."
—Miley Cyrus, singer and actor

What does this quote mean to you?

"Mistakes are always forgivable if one has the courage to admit them."
—Bruce Lee, actor, director, and martial artist

What does this quote mean to you?

"We don't make mistakes, just happy little accidents."
—Bob Ross, painter

What does this quote mean to you?

"Anyone who has never made a mistake has never tried anything new."
—Albert Einstein, scientist

What does this quote mean to you?

Dear Mistake

Our mistakes deserve a thank-you for all they have taught us! Write a letter to a mistake that you have made. Tell your mistake what you learned from it and how it helped you become even more awesome.

Dear _ ,

_ _

_ _

_ _

_ _

_ _

_ _

_ _

_ _

Sincerely,

_ _

It's okay to feel frustrated sometimes

Even though you know how great mistakes can be and you've learned strategies to use your mistakes to help you, you might still feel frustrated sometimes. That's okay! It's normal to feel frustrated when you are working on learning something new. What's important is how you choose to deal with that frustration.

Sometimes when people get frustrated, they feel like giving up. Now that we are working toward a growth mindset, we know that giving up is not for us. Pushing through challenges, even when it feels impossible, is called **perseverance**. Part of having a growth mindset is practicing perseverance. You might be thinking, "I know I'm supposed to keep trying, but sometimes I just get *so* frustrated that I can't even think anymore!" Well, don't worry, there are a lot of strategies for dealing with your frustration in a way that will allow you to keep pushing forward.

TAKE A LOOK AT THESE STRATEGIES FOR DEALING WITH FRUSTRATION:

Take a break. It's okay to take a break when you feel like your brain can't handle any more working! Choose an activity that will allow your brain to think about something else for a while. Here are some ways to take a break that will help your brain refocus and reenergize.

- **Eat a healthy snack.** Healthy foods give our brain the energy it needs to think and work through problems.
- **Exercise.** Going for a walk or playing your favorite sport can help calm and refocus your mind.
- **Listen to your favorite song.** Music can improve your mood, which can help take away the frustration you are feeling.
- **Do something creative.** Creative activities, such as drawing, completing a craft, or writing, are good for giving the creative part of your brain some exercise. This will help you with **problem solving** when you get back to work.

Practice mindfulness. When you focus on the present moment, you are practicing **mindfulness.** This practice quiets your mind and calms your body. Mindfulness is a great way to manage frustration because it allows you to pay attention to what's happening *right now*, instead of worrying about a difficult task or how to fix your mistake. Try these simple mindfulness exercises and notice how your body and mind feel afterward.

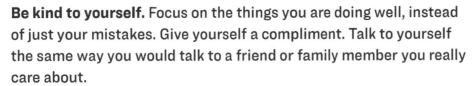

- **Belly breaths:** Lie on your back and place your hands flat on your belly. Take deep breaths in through your nose and out of your mouth. Watch the way your hands rise and fall on your belly.
- **5-4-3-2-1:** Notice five things you see, four things you feel, three things you hear, two things you smell, and one thing you taste.

Be kind to yourself. Focus on the things you are doing well, instead of just your mistakes. Give yourself a compliment. Talk to yourself the same way you would talk to a friend or family member you really care about.

You're ready to try some exercises to deal with frustration. Remember, you can always come back to this section of the book when you need help calming your mind and body down so you can persevere!

Next Time . . .

Last night at basketball practice, I missed all my free-throw shots. I was so frustrated, I stormed off the court and refused to finish practice. I just didn't feel like doing it anymore! Next time, I will take a break for five minutes to focus on my breathing and calm my body down, then try again.

Positive Affirmations

Positive affirmations can help us manage feelings of frustration and self-doubt. An **affirmation** is something we can say to ourselves to offer encouragement and self-love. It is a reminder that we are doing a great job. Repeating positive affirmations to ourselves can help us manage our frustration in a safe and healthy way and get us back on track to try again.

Try saying some of these affirmations out loud to yourself:

- I am smarter than my mistakes.
- I can persevere through any challenge.
- I am choosing to strengthen my brain.
- I am capable of great things.
- I am proud of the work I have done so far.

Now write two of your own affirmations to yourself.

1. _____

2. _____

Keep On Rolling

For this exercise, you will need a paper clip and a pencil. Place your paper clip in the center of the wheel. Put the tip of your pencil inside the end of your paper clip, at the center of the wheel, to hold the clip in place. Flick the paper clip to make it spin around the wheel. Complete whichever exercise it lands on. You can go back to "It's okay to feel frustrated" (see page 38) to remind yourself how to do the mindfulness practices. Still feeling frustrated? Try another one!

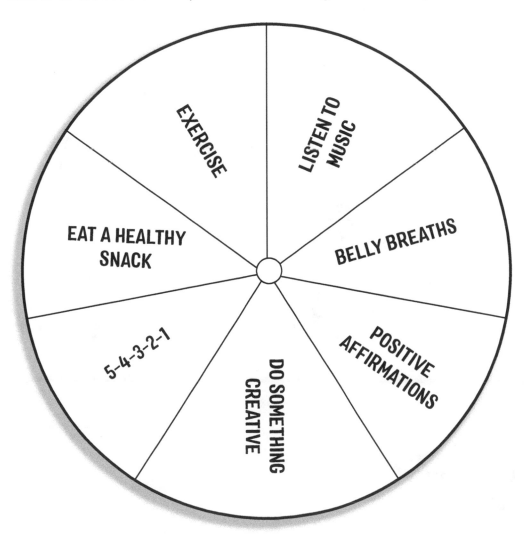

The wheel contains these sections: EXERCISE, LISTEN TO MUSIC, BELLY BREATHS, POSITIVE AFFIRMATIONS, DO SOMETHING CREATIVE, 5-4-3-2-1, EAT A HEALTHY SNACK

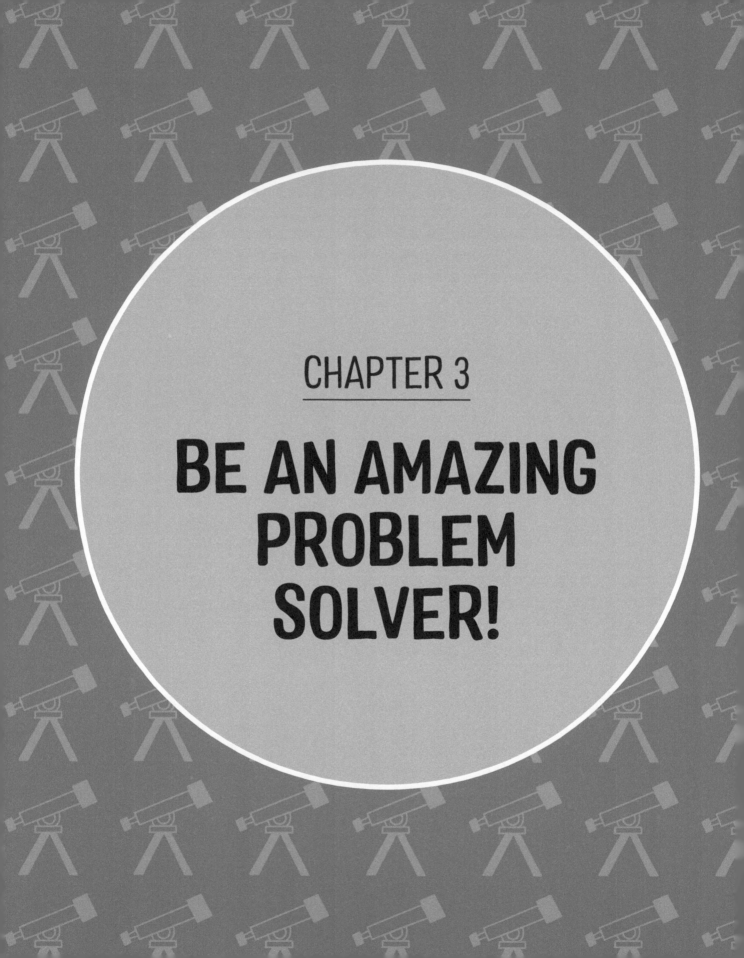

CHAPTER 3

BE AN AMAZING PROBLEM SOLVER!

A big part of developing your growth mindset is learning how to be an amazing problem solver. It's not just about learning from your mistakes—it's also about thinking up new strategies for doing things differently to improve or fix your mistakes. Each time you try something new, you get closer and closer to solving your problem, which is why problem solving can be so much fun! Many problems have more than one solution. When you are solving problems, you get to use your **creativity** to come up with all the possible solutions. We can learn to love a challenge the same way we have learned to love our mistakes. In this chapter, you will explore what it means to be an amazing problem solver by taking feedback, embracing challenges, and using the powerful word "yet." Let's get started by looking at some different types of problems we can solve and how we can work toward finding solutions for them.

More than just math problems

When you think about solving a problem, you might think about the math problems you solve at school. You've probably learned all kinds of strategies to solve different types of math problems. So you have already practiced problem solving! But problem solving is so much more than just math problems. In fact, you solve problems every single day. **Problem solving** is the process of finding a solution to an issue.

In addition to academic problems, like math questions or science experiments, you can use problem solving for conflicts, like with your friends or family. Think about a time when a friend was upset with you about something. You probably thought about what happened to cause it and tried to come up with a way to fix it to make your friend happy again. That's problem solving!

Before you can solve your problem, it's important to be sure you really understand exactly what the problem is. Here are some questions you can ask to make sure you understand what you are trying to solve.

- When did the problem start?

- How did I notice the problem?

- What are some possible causes for the problem?

- What have I already tried? Why didn't that work?

- Has this happened before? If so, how did I solve it then?

- What happens if I ignore this problem?

- What are the facts that I *know* about this problem?

- Who could possibly help me solve this problem?

There are some things that can keep us from solving our problems.

THINGS TO AVOID:

- Giving up too early
- Having a negative attitude or engaging in negative **self-talk**
- Thinking you already know everything
- Not taking time to understand your problem
- Refusing to ask for help

Part of problem solving means having an open mind and being willing to try different things. The first solution you try might not work, so having a strategy, or a plan of action, before you start is helpful. It is best to be prepared with multiple ideas for solving the problem. Sometimes this means using your creativity to think about the problem in different ways and trying different things until the right solution comes along. Don't forget to use your mistakes to help you!

The next three exercises will help you become an expert in thinking like a problem solver!

My Problem Plan

Think about a problem you are having right now. This could be a problem at school, at home, with a friend, or in an extracurricular activity.

My problem:

Take a look at these possible solutions and make a plan to solve your problem.

- Learn more about my problem.
- Apologize.
- Ask for advice.
- Practice a skill that will help me solve my problem.
- Try to better understand what my problem is.
- Ask questions about my problem.
- Do some research about similar problems.
- Talk to a trusted adult.
- Take action to fix a mistake.

To solve my problem, I will try

If that doesn't work, I will try

If I still haven't solved my problem, I will

More Than One Solution

Many problems have more than one solution. That's why it's important to think of all the possible solutions when you are problem solving. These problems have more than one answer. Try them!

1. _ _ _ _ _ _ _ _ + _ _ _ _ _ _ _ _ _ _ + _ _ _ _ _ _ _ _ _ = 100

   What could the solution be? _ _ _ _ _ _ _ _, _ _ _ _ _ _ _ _ _ _, _ _ _ _ _ _ _ _ _ _

   What is another solution? _ _ _ _ _ _ _ _ _ _, _ _ _ _ _ _ _ _ _ _, _ _ _ _ _ _ _ _ _

2. Draw a garden. Half the flowers are red.

What could the garden look like? What's another possible solution?

3. The answer is "triangle."
   What could the question be?

   _

   What other question could it be?

   _

Advice for a Friend

Give advice to each friend in the following examples to help them solve their problem. Remember to think of multiple solutions and be encouraging.

1. Your friend is failing social studies. There is one test left before report cards come out. What is your advice to your friend?

   ----

2. Two of your friends are in an argument. One friend gave the other friend her favorite pencil, then decided she wanted it back, but the other friend won't give it back. What is your advice to your friends?

   ----

3. Your friend is always late for school because she doesn't wake up in time and misses the bus. If she is tardy one more time, there will be a consequence. What is your advice to your friend?

   ----

4. Your friend is working on a project for the science fair. He keeps trying the same thing over and over again, and it isn't working. He is *sure* it's the right way. What is your advice to your friend?

Taking feedback

Mei's teacher told her the reason she wasn't doing well on her math quizzes was that she was always talking to her friend during the lessons. At first Mei felt angry, but she thought about it and knew her teacher was right, so she started practicing self-control in class and her grades improved.

Ben's football coach told him if he wanted to play in the games, he needed to participate more during practice. Ben was furious and thought his coach just didn't like him, so he ignored this advice. He wasn't allowed to play in the next game.

Think about each of the stories above. How did each person feel when someone gave them a suggestion? Which person listened to feedback? Which person had success?

Feedback is information that a person gives you to help you improve. It can be really hard to hear sometimes, because it doesn't feel good when someone tells you that you are doing something wrong or that you could be doing better. It's normal to feel this way. But most of the time, feedback is given in order to help you. The person giving you information about how to improve usually just wants you to be successful!

When a person has a fixed mindset, they might want to ignore feedback, get angry, or make excuses. Part of having a growth mindset is welcoming feedback and using it to help you. Having suggestions from other people can be a powerful tool! You will often get feedback from parents, teachers, coaches, or other adults whose job it is to help you succeed. Listen to this feedback with an open mind and use it as a tool to change and grow.

HERE ARE SOME HELPFUL TIPS FOR TAKING FEEDBACK:

- Listen closely with an open mind.
- Notice how the feedback makes you feel.
- Ask yourself why it makes you feel that way.
- If you feel upset, take a moment to calm down.
- Restate what the person said and ask if you are understanding correctly.
- Remind yourself that they are trying to help you.
- Thank the person for wanting to help you succeed.
- Brainstorm ways you can use the feedback to be more successful.
- Take action!

Next Time...

At parent-teacher conferences, my teacher told me I would be more successful in class if I asked questions when I was confused about something. The next time I don't understand something, I will raise my hand and ask a question.

Feedback Mindset

Look at each example of a person reacting to feedback they were given. Decide whether this person is showing a growth mindset or a fixed mindset. Circle the correct answer.

"This person just doesn't like me."	(fixed mindset)	growth mindset
"This person wants to help me succeed."	fixed mindset	(growth mindset)
"Now you try."	fixed mindset	growth mindset
"He is just jealous of me."	fixed mindset	growth mindset
"I should listen to this advice to get better."	fixed mindset	growth mindset
"Feedback helps me grow."	fixed mindset	growth mindset
"I don't care what she says."	fixed mindset	growth mindset
"I don't have to listen to anyone."	fixed mindset	growth mindset
"I'll think about how this could help me."	fixed mindset	growth mindset
"I'll just ignore what she is saying."	fixed mindset	growth mindset
"No matter what he says, I'll never be good."	fixed mindset	growth mindset

Think, Restate, Thank, Decide

In this exercise, you will practice responding to feedback using these four steps:

Step 1: <u>Think</u> about what the person said.

Step 2: <u>Restate</u> it in your own words to show you understand.

Step 3: <u>Thank</u> them for giving you helpful feedback.

Step 4: <u>Decide</u> how you will use it.

Think about feedback you have been given by a parent, teacher, coach, or friend. It could be about your work in school, sports, the way you treat others, or your behavior.

Follow the four steps to respond to the feedback.

My feedback was

- -

Step 1:

- -

Step 2:

- -

Step 3:

- -

Step 4:

- -

Always improving!

When you have a growth mindset, you are always improving. Many times, it takes more than one try to get something right. Think about when you were learning to read. You didn't just pick up a book one day and know all the words in it. You probably started by listening to someone else read to you. Then you had to learn all the letters and all the sounds each letter makes. After you knew the letters and their sounds, you learned how to put them together to make words. You started to read short words and then short sentences. You probably used different strategies, like looking at the pictures or breaking words apart and sounding them out. Next, you probably started reading longer sentences and then longer books. The more you practiced reading, and the more strategies you tried, the more you improved. And now you're reading this book! But what if you had stopped after the first try because it was hard? What if you had never picked up another book again?

Just like with learning to read, accomplishing our goals and trying new things doesn't always work out on the first try. Part of having a growth mindset is understanding that even if you don't succeed the first time, you will improve with each try. It's important to remember that word "perseverance," which we learned in chapter 2. If we push through our challenges, we will continue to improve. Think about how much you've improved your growth mindset just by working through this book!

Let's review the science behind how our brains grow: When the neurons in your brain are challenged, they make new connections and become stronger. That's why things get a little bit easier each time you try. Your brain is slowly becoming ready for the new skill. It just takes time, practice, and a growth mindset!

As you complete the next few exercises, think about why having a growth mindset helps you keep improving. Be sure to take some time to celebrate all the ways you have improved through hard work and perseverance.

Better Today

Think of all the ways you have improved over the past year! Make a list of things you are better at today than you were last year.

1. _____

2. _____

3. _____

4. _____

5. _____

Look How I've Grown!

Improving isn't always easy. It takes a lot of work. But think about how great it feels when you grow and achieve your goals. Reflect on something you have had to work really hard at and how you improved over time. How did it feel? What did you have to do to get there? Write about it. Be sure to congratulate yourself for how hard you've worked!

_____

_____

_____

_____

_____

_____

A-*Maze*-ing Improvement

Try this tricky maze without erasing!

Did you get better? Try it again!

Try it again, and notice how you improve.

Just like with the maze, we aren't always successful on the first try. Sometimes we don't even get it right by the third try! But the more we try, the closer we get to success!

Don't you love a challenge?

The human brain was built to learn and grow. There is no limit to all the things you can learn and do when you have a growth mindset! Loving challenges and learning will help you become a lifelong learner to achieve your biggest goals. Facing problems or challenges can be frustrating and might even make you want to give up, but you have learned strategies to keep pushing forward. With all the strategies you have learned to help you persevere, you can actually come to love a challenge instead of feeling frustrated or defeated by it.

HERE ARE SOME STRATEGIES FOR EMBRACING CHALLENGES AND LEARNING:

Try doing challenging things instead of avoiding them. When you avoid difficult things, you don't allow yourself the chance to grow. Doing something poorly and learning from it is better than not doing it at all.

Don't label yourself "good" or "bad." Forget about the things you think you are "bad" at. Instead, see them as challenges that you get to overcome. Don't assume you aren't cut out for a certain skill. Focus on the room to grow instead of the times you have struggled.

Figure out your motivation. Decide *why* you want to get through a challenge or learn a skill. How will it help you in the future? Figuring out this motivation will help you feel excited to learn and work toward your goals.

Understand how you learn best. We all have different styles of learning. Figuring out which one works best for you can help you love learning and tackling your challenges. Some people learn best by seeing examples, and others learn best by listening. Others learn best by doing and learning from their mistakes as they go. You might learn best using more than one of these styles.

Celebrate your successes. Trying new things and overcoming challenges takes hard work, so it's important to congratulate yourself when you make progress or achieve something new. Find ways to reward yourself and be proud of your hard work.

Instead of seeing your challenges as roadblocks standing in your way, you can think of them as exciting steps along your journey to becoming an even smarter and more capable person. If something is going to help you get closer to your goals, why not love it? The following exercises will help you think about what challenges you and how you can begin to love tackling those challenges.

Next Time . . .

I used to avoid math because I always felt like I just wasn't a "math person." I never understood it as quickly as my classmates. I decided to look at math as a fun challenge to tackle, because I know my brain can grow when I work hard. Next time I struggle with something in school, I'll have the same attitude to make learning fun.

What Challenges Me?

It's important to know what skills challenge us so we can begin to think about how to tackle them. Take a look at each skill and circle the ones that challenge you most.

READING	TEAMWORK	SINGING
SELF-CONTROL	WRITING	GETTING ALONG WITH OTHERS
ART	LISTENING	FOLLOWING DIRECTIONS
SCIENCE	MATH	BEING ON TIME
MAKING FRIENDS	DANCING	SPORTS
PLAYING AN INSTRUMENT	SPEAKING IN FRONT OF A GROUP	FOCUSING
COMPUTER SKILLS	PROBLEM SOLVING	ORGANIZATION

Choose one of the challenges you circled. How can you take steps to begin to tackle it?

Just Like the Movies

Just as we face challenges, the characters in movies, TV shows, and books face challenges that they have to overcome, too. Think about a character who inspired you by overcoming a challenge. Write about the problem the character faced, how the character overcame it, and why that character inspired you.

Learning to Love It

Think about a subject or skill that you struggle with in school or dread learning about.

What is the subject or skill?

_ _

What do you dislike about it?

_ _

_ _

What is one thing you do like about it?

_ _

What would make this subject or skill more fun?

_ _

_ _

How could you take actions to make it more enjoyable for you?

_ _

_ _

_ _

Whenever you feel like you are facing a challenge in school or aren't enjoying learning about something, come back to this exercise and brainstorm about how to love learning about it!

"Yet" is a powerful word

"I can't run a mile without stopping."

"I can't run a mile without stopping . . . yet."

Read these two sentences. What is different about them? Which one do you think was said by a person with a growth mindset? Which one shows a fixed mindset?

The two sentences have all the same words except one. That word is "yet" and it is extremely powerful. That one word changes the whole meaning! If someone says they can't run a mile without stopping, it sounds like they believe they won't ever be able to do it, or that they don't have a positive mindset about it. It is a limiting statement, which means it can keep a person from reaching their goals or becoming the best version of themselves. When the word "yet" is added to the sentence, it opens up possibilities for success.

Think about a baby who is learning how to walk. What if the first time the baby fell, they never got up and tried again? Babies are great examples of the power of "yet" because they keep trying even when something is hard. Babies aren't scared of failing or being embarrassed by not being able to do something. As we grow older, we start to worry about what other people might think or how we will feel about ourselves if we fail. Letting go of fear and self-doubt can be hard, but using the word "yet" is a great start!

When you feel like saying "I can't" or "I don't know how," try adding that one simple word to the end of it. "I can't . . . YET." Adding "yet" means you will keep trying, no matter how hard it is. It means you believe in yourself enough to persevere. We know that part of having a growth mindset is believing we always have the ability to improve. Using the word "yet" is a way to communicate to others, and, most important, to ourselves, that we have a growth mindset. The next few exercises will help you practice the power of "yet."

Next Time . . .

"I can't do it!" The next time you feel like you are struggling with something, what powerful word will you add to the end of this sentence to change your thinking?

Things I Can't Do ... Yet

Make a list of three things you can already do.

1. _____

2. _____

3. _____

Congratulate yourself for already being able to do these things! Now think of three things that you can't do . . . YET. Remember to use that powerful word at the end of your statements.

1. _____

2. _____

3. _____

Congratulate yourself for having the mindset to work toward accomplishing these things!

Use What You've Got

Think about all the talents you already have (including the three you listed in the last exercise). How can you use the things you can do well to help you accomplish one of the things that you can't do yet? Choose one thing that you'd like to get better at and write about how your current skills and talents can help you achieve it.

You're Right!

"Whether you think you can, or you think you can't—you're right."
—Henry Ford, businessperson

What does this quote mean to you? How does it explain the power of "yet"?

CHAPTER 4

GET CREATIVE AND KEEP TRYING!

Sometimes problem solving and working through challenges takes some creativity. This chapter will help you understand how creativity and hard work go together to help you achieve amazing things. You have learned how important it is to keep trying, even when things get hard. Sometimes you might feel like you've tried everything and you don't know what to do next. That's when you can really tap into your creativity! The exercises in this chapter will teach you how to think outside the box and make a plan to achieve your goals. You'll also learn that with practice, there are no limits to all the awesome things you can do! Put on your creative-thinking cap and get ready to dive in.

Tap into your creativity

Creativity is your ability to think of things in new and different ways. When you think of the word "creativity," you might think about art. Artists use creativity to make new things and to see things in a different way. But you don't have to be an artist to be creative! The truth is, creativity can actually apply to anything. You might not realize it yet, but you already use your creativity all the time. When we start trying to be creative on purpose, by tapping into our creativity, we become better at learning and problem solving.

   If you aren't sure if you're creative, take a look at this list. If you've done any of these things, you were using creativity!

- Taking things apart and putting them back together
- Making something new
- Using your imagination
- Solving a problem
- Figuring out how to do something new
- Pretending

Have you ever heard the phrase "think outside the box"? This is another way of talking about thinking creatively. It's important to be able to think outside the box because it helps us come up with *all* the possible solutions to a problem and *all* the new things we can create. Creative thinking is part of having a growth mindset because it helps you tackle problems in many different ways and allows you to imagine all the possibilities. Someone with a fixed mindset would likely give up after trying one strategy or solution. With a growth mindset, we know we can use our creative thinking to keep working on our problem.

HERE ARE SOME TIPS FOR THINKING OUTSIDE THE BOX:

Ask lots of questions. When you are wondering about something, ask! **Curiosity** is great for our creative side.

Try new things. When you have new experiences, the neurons in your brain form new connections. These connections allow you to use more parts of your brain, which is great for creativity!

Keep an open mind. Be accepting of the idea that there is more than one solution. Being creative means exploring many possibilities, even the ones that don't seem obvious.

Learn how things work. How does a television work? How are cars made? When you understand the process of how different things work, you can combine ideas to create something new or fix something old.

Create things. Draw, build, write, and design. All these are great practice for our creativity.

Keep a list of your ideas. Any time you have a creative idea, write it down! Go back and look at it when you need to spark some creativity.

Play and pretend. Sometimes as we get older, we stop using our imaginations as much when we play, but doing so is *great* for practicing creative thinking!

Use these tips and your own special creativity to complete the following exercises and become an expert at tapping into your creative side.

Draw Outside the Box

Look at the lines and shapes in the following boxes. Use your creativity to add on to the existing lines or shapes to create a picture.

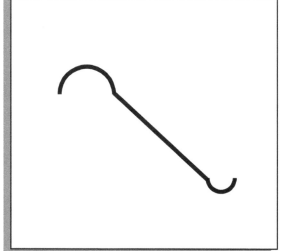

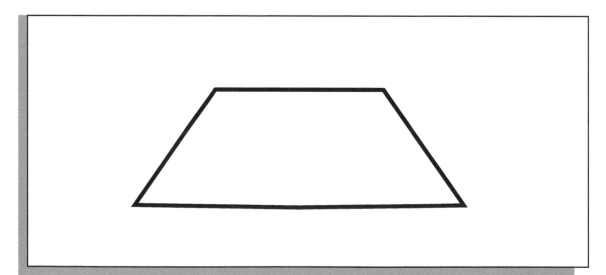

This Used to Be a . . .

In this exercise, you will look at different everyday items and decide what you could turn them into. A great example of this is a tire swing. It started as just a regular tire that someone had on their car, then a creative person thought to turn it into a swing! Use your creativity to think outside the box and come up with other uses for these objects.

This used to be a flowerpot.

Now it's a _ _ _ _ _ _ _ _ _ _ _ _ _ _ _ _ _ .

This used to be an umbrella.

Now it's a _ _ _ _ _ _ _ _ _ _ _ _ _ _ _ _ _ .

This used to be a pencil.

Now it's a _ _ _ _ _ _ _ _ _ _ _ _ _ _ _ _ _ .

This used to be a trash can.

Now it's a _ _ _ _ _ _ _ _ _ _ _ _ _ _ _ _ _ .

Silly Solutions

In this exercise, you will use your creativity to think of how you could use a set of items to solve a problem or create something new. Sometimes being creative means getting silly!

1. How could you use a skateboard, a laundry basket, and a jump rope to make it easier to take out the trash?

   ----

2. How could you use a mixing bowl, a trampoline, and a ball of yarn to rescue a cat stuck in a tree?

   ----

3. How could you use a trash can, a flip-flop, and some jelly beans to create a new game?

Practice, practice, practice

In third grade, Miguel struggled with remembering multiplication facts, and he knew it was important for him to know them to do well in fourth grade. He spent the summer practicing for 15 minutes every day, and by the first day of fourth grade, he could answer all the questions about them correctly.

Jayla had to give a speech in front of her class for a social studies assignment, but she was very nervous. Her grandmother told her that practicing her speech over and over would help her be more comfortable when it came time to speak to the class. She practiced each night leading up to the big day. Eventually she knew every word of the speech, and her grandmother was right!

Miguel and Jayla both learned how important practice is. They both put in the time and effort to improve at a skill and be prepared. But why is practice so important, and how does it work? We know that learning a new skill creates new connections between neurons in our brains. Each time we practice that skill, the neural connection gets stronger and stronger. The stronger the connection is, the easier the skill becomes!

Practice for short periods of time. When we try to practice a skill for hours at a time, our bodies and brains can get tired, and the practice won't be as effective or helpful. Instead, try practicing for short periods of time.

Practice often. Practicing only a few times or with long intervals between practices won't strengthen the connection between neurons in the brain. Try to practice as often as possible. Set a schedule for yourself and stick to it.

Break it up. Find a way to break up the skill into smaller chunks. For example, if you are learning multiplication facts, don't try to learn them all at once. Start with one set of facts, and when you know all of them, move on to the next set.

Do it right. Make sure you are doing the skill you are practicing *correctly*. If you practice something the wrong way over and over again, the incorrect way will stick.

Repetition is important. Doing the same thing over and over again can seem boring or even silly, but repetition is the best way to strengthen those connections in your brain.

Make it fun! When you find ways to make practice enjoyable, you will be more motivated to stick with it. Turn your practice into a game or find friends to practice with. Use your creative brain to make it fun.

Keep these strategies in mind while you work through the next few exercises!

Let's Do It Again . . . and Again!

Doing something more than once helps you improve. Look at this drawing of a pig, then try to draw it in first box. Don't worry about making it perfect—just do your best!

How did you do? Which part was the most challenging?

Let's see how practicing can improve your work. Draw it again in the second box. After you are finished, look at your drawing and see how you can improve it even more. Draw it one more time in the third box. Try to get it as close to the original picture as possible.

Reflect: How did your drawing change each time?

Did it get easier or harder each time? Explain.

Do you think it's important to try things more than once? Why or why not?

To My Friend Who Doesn't Practice

Imagine you have a friend who doesn't understand the importance and value of practice. Write an encouraging letter to this person, explaining why practice is important and giving suggestions for strategies. Tell them about a time when you got better at something by practicing.

Dear Friend Who Doesn't Practice,

Sincerely,

Making a plan

"A goal without a plan is just a wish." These words from French writer Antoine de Saint-Exupéry describe just how important it is to have a plan when you are working toward achieving something. Having a plan gives you small, achievable steps that help move you toward your end goal. Let's talk about why this is important.

When you set a new goal or work to solve a new problem, it can seem overwhelming at first. You know what you want to achieve, but how exactly are you going to get there? Where should you start? How long is it going to take? Making a plan answers all (or most) of these questions and gives you a clear path to success!

Imagine that your PE teacher wants everyone in your class to be able to run a mile in 9 minutes by the end of the school year. Imagine that you've never been a runner, so this feels like a problem for you, and you know you need to start slowly. Here is an example of how you could break this goal into steps.

Step 1: Walk 1 mile.

Step 2: Walk ¼ mile. Run ¼ mile. Walk ¼ mile. Run ¼ mile.

Step 3: Walk ½ mile. Run ½ mile.

Step 4: Walk ¼ mile. Run ¾ mile.

Step 5: Run 1 mile in 13 minutes.

Step 6: Run 1 mile in 11 minutes.

Step 7: Run 1 mile in 9 minutes.

You did it!

Notice how the steps change each time. You can see that the plan doesn't just jump straight from "Walk 1 mile" to "Run ½ mile." That would be hard to achieve without the smaller step in between. When you try to move too quickly to your goal, you are likely to get frustrated. You might even get discouraged and want to give up. When you set small steps to achieve your goals, you can make slow and steady progress and feel good about your achievements along the way. You can also set a specific amount of time for each goal. For example, if your goal is to run 1 mile in 9 minutes by the end of the school year, you might choose to devote one month to each step and plan to practice three to four times a week. Setting an amount of time for each step can help keep you on track.

Next Time . . .

I'm on the track team, and I wanted to become a faster runner. I went to practice every day, but my speed was staying the same. My coach talked to me about making a plan with gradual, small steps to increase my speed. I worked on one step at a time, and noticed my speed starting to increase. The next time I have a goal, I will make a plan with slow, small steps.

The next few exercises will help you practice looking at your goal or problem, breaking it down into steps, and coming up with a **long-term solution** instead of a quick fix.

Think Before You Plan

It is important to take time to think about your problem or goal before you make your action steps. You need to understand the problem or goal and predict any roadblocks that you might come to while working on your plan. Take time to reflect on your problem or goal to make sure you really understand it. Here are some questions you can ask yourself.

- What am I trying to solve or achieve?
- Why do I want to solve or achieve this?
- What is causing this problem?
- What will happen if I do nothing?
- When did my problem start?
- What have I already tried? What worked and what didn't?
- What facts do I know about this problem or goal?
- Who can help me with this problem or goal?
- How long will it take to solve my problem or reach my goal?
- Has this problem happened before? What did I do?
- How have I achieved goals in the past?

After you have reflected on some of these questions, write about a problem or goal you have. Be sure to answer at least three of the questions in your response.

Break It Down

Think about each goal or problem and how you can break it down into five smaller steps.

You have a piano recital coming up and you need to learn (and be ready to perform) three new songs.

Step 1: _____

Step 2: _____

Step 3: _____

Step 4: _____

Step 5: _____

You are working on a project for your social studies class. You have to write an essay and create a presentation. You get to choose the topic. It's due in one week.

Step 1: _____

Step 2: _____

Step 3: _____

Step 4: _____

Step 5: _____

You are on the basketball team and you want to improve your free-throw shooting before the tournament in four weeks. Right now you are making one out of every ten shots. You want to make eight out of every ten.

Step 1: _____

Step 2: _____

Step 3: _____

Step 4: _____

Step 5: _____

You are in the school play and you have to memorize all your lines. There are three acts in the play, and you have ten lines in each act. You want to have them all memorized by the first rehearsal in five weeks.

Step 1: _____

Step 2: _____

Step 3: _____

Step 4: _____

Step 5: _____

More Than a Band-Aid

When you are solving a problem, it's important to consider whether the solution is a long-term solution or just a quick fix. A quick fix is a solution that will hide the problem or only help for a short time, but not actually solve it. It is much better to have a long-term solution, one that will keep the problem from coming back up. Read each example of a solution to a problem. Color the solutions that won't solve the problem over the long term **red**. Color the helpful long-term solutions **green**.

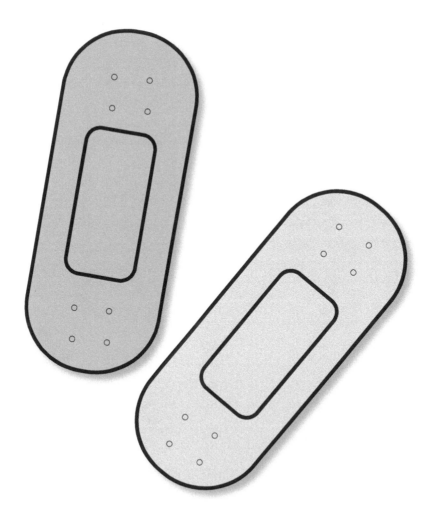

You broke your mom's favorite mug, so you hide the pieces behind the couch so she won't see.

You need money to pay for your summer camp. You just used all of yours on a new video game, so you borrow it from your big brother, but you don't have a plan to pay him back.

Your new dog is chewing on everything in the house. You take her to a dog trainer and work with her every day to train her to stop.

Your parents tell you that you can't play with the neighbors until your homework is finished. You tell them it's finished, even though it really isn't. You spend the rest of the afternoon playing.

You are struggling with math at school this year. You decide to start working with a tutor every week to help you learn.

Your dentist tells you that you have cavities from all the sugar you are eating. You decide to limit your desserts to three times a week instead of every day.

Your dad asks you to clean your room. You don't feel like doing it right now, so you shove everything under your bed.

You learn about the importance of exercise in health class. You haven't really been exercising, so you decide to start joining your mom on her evening walk every night.

No limits!

Having a growth mindset means believing there are no limits to all the great things you can do. When you start to think, "I can't do that," ignore those silly limiting thoughts and use your creative thinking instead! Creative thinking allows you to come up with new strategies for tackling problems or achieving goals with *no limits*.

Achieving a goal or solving a problem feels great, and you should take time to celebrate your accomplishments. You deserve it. But don't stop there! When you have a growth mindset, you are always thinking about ways to grow *even more*. So after you celebrate your success, start **brainstorming** about how you can expand on it. What's next? How can you take it a step further? What else do you want to achieve? What did you learn from your last problem or goal that can help you do even more with it? These are great questions to ask yourself as you brainstorm.

If you come up with an idea and then think, "There's *no way* I can do that," check your mindset. A growth mindset means there aren't limits to how much you can learn and grow as long as you are willing to use your creative brain and work hard. When you feel like you can't do something, remember that creative thinking can be a powerful tool. Let's say you have a goal to help out a homeless shelter by donating $1,000. What a great goal! But you may say to yourself, "I'm just a kid, and I don't have a job! I don't have $1,000! I guess I'll have to wait to achieve this goal when I'm a grown-up." *That* is a limiting belief! Your creative brain can come up with strategies to make this happen *now.* You could host a bake sale, ask local businesses for donations, get friends involved, and so much more. Instead of thinking, "Here's why I can't do that . . . ," start thinking, "Here's how I *can* do that. . . ."

If you try one idea and it doesn't work, don't stop there. Think about how you could improve that idea and make changes to it. If it still doesn't work, try another idea. Having no limits means you are always thinking of what else you can do and not giving up when things get hard.

The next two exercises will help you practice believing in yourself and examine the importance of not giving up.

Saying Is Believing

The more we say positive things to ourselves, the more we believe them. The same is true about negative things, which is why it is so important to avoid negative self-talk. Sometimes when we are working on solving a problem or achieving a goal, we get frustrated and start to put ourselves down. You can try this exercise when you notice that happening to you.

1. Find a mirror and look into it.

2. Look at yourself with a feeling of love.

3. Say your biggest dream out loud to yourself.

4. Choose a positive affirmation to say out loud to yourself:

   ❑   I can push past any obstacles in my way.

   ❑   I will overcome challenges to meet my goal.

   ❑   I can do amazing things.

   ❑   I am strong and capable of great success.

   ❑   I am brave for trying something new.

   ❑   I am proud of myself for working hard.

   ❑   I love myself for working to improve.

Reflect: How did you feel after completing this exercise?

What If They Had Given Up?

J. K. Rowling, the author of the *Harry Potter* series, was going through a hard time when she started writing those famous books. She had just gotten a divorce and was barely able to afford food for herself and her baby. She sent the book to many publishers and it was rejected each time.

What if J. K. Rowling had given up?

Thomas Edison, inventor of the light bulb, struggled when he was in school. His teachers even told him that he wasn't smart enough to learn anything. He also struggled when he worked on his inventions, failing hundreds of times, and even getting fired from his first two jobs.

What if Thomas Edison had given up?

Michael Jordan, the former NBA player who is often referred to as the best basketball player of all time, didn't make his high school varsity basketball team.

What if Michael Jordan had given up?

CHAPTER 5

SET GOALS, AND THEN SET MORE GOALS!

You have learned all about the power of a growth mindset, how awesome mistakes are, and how to persevere through problems using creative thinking. Now that you know all the amazing things you are capable of, it's time to set some goals! A goal is a wish or desire that is put into action through a plan. In this chapter, you will learn why goals are important, how to begin thinking about goals, how to put a plan into action, and what to do once you have achieved a goal. The exercises will give you practice in brainstorming, reflecting, and taking action. By the end of this chapter, you will be ready to dive right into goal setting and tackling a plan to achieve great things!

Why do you want to do things?

We've talked a little bit about setting goals, but what's the point of it? The best-performing athletes, entertainers, and businesspeople all set goals for themselves. Why do you think these people set goals? Why do *you* want to set goals?

There are a lot of reasons to set goals. Take a look at these important benefits of goal setting:

Goals make you accountable. When you are **accountable** for something, you are responsible for it and are expected to get it done. Having a goal helps keep you accountable to complete the actions you need to achieve it. Sharing your goal with others also allows them to help keep you accountable.

Goals keep you focused. Setting a clear goal with a plan helps keep you focused on the things you need to be working on to achieve what you want.

Goals can motivate you. Having a goal can help motivate you to stay on track to accomplish it. It feels good to achieve a goal.

Goals help you become a better version of yourself. When you are working toward a goal, you are improving a skill and becoming a better person than you were yesterday.

Goals can come in all shapes and sizes, which means different goals take different amounts of time. Think about these two goals:

1. I will learn to do long division.
2. I will become a chemist.

What is different about these two goals? You probably guessed that it will take much longer to become a chemist than it will to learn long division, and you are right. Both of these are great goals, but each one will take a different amount of planning. People have **long-term goals**, like becoming a chemist, that may take years of planning and action. You can also have **short-term goals** that may take anywhere from a few days to a few months of planning and action. It's good to have both types of goals!

In the following exercises, you will reflect on the importance of goals and practice setting some for yourself. Let's get started!

A World Without Goals

Imagine *no one* had ever set a goal. What would the world be like if there were no goals?

Wheel of Fortune

Fill in each section of the wheel with a goal you have in that area of your life. Think about how you can take steps to achieve these goals.

Wouldn't it be so great if . . .

Fill in the blank. Wouldn't it be so great if I _____?

Imagine yourself achieving your goal. What do you see? How do you feel? Are you proud of yourself? Who is celebrating with you? Reaching a goal is such a rewarding feeling. It takes hard work and should be celebrated! Imagining what reaching your goals would look and feel like can be really motivating. When you start to feel frustrated by challenges or mistakes (remember, both are amazing!) as you work toward your goal, it can be helpful to stop and take a minute to visualize yourself achieving that goal. We'll practice this some more in the following exercises.

It can be helpful to know what your strengths and areas for improvement are. However, when it comes to goals, you don't want to hold yourself back by only focusing on what you think your strengths are. Our challenges are sometimes just strengths waiting to happen! Having a growth mindset reminds us that challenges are opportunities for growth. Sometimes, with a goal and some hard work, we can turn our challenges into strengths. Our goals should include both our strengths and our challenges so we don't limit ourselves from trying new things and improving from growth.

Here's an example: Kayden is great at playing the guitar. Playing the piano is a lot harder for him, but he really enjoys it. He wants to set some goals for himself to improve his musical talents. He knows he's already really good at guitar, so he wonders if he should set a goal to learn new songs on the guitar, since that is his strength. If he focuses only on his strength (playing the guitar), he will limit himself from what he enjoys (playing the piano). Instead of setting a goal only for his strength, he could set a goal to play three new songs on the guitar *and* three new songs on the piano.

In the next two exercises, you will practice imagining yourself reaching your goal. Notice how great it feels and remember not to let your ideas about what your strengths are limit you!

I Can See It Now . . .

Visualization is our ability to create pictures in our mind. When we visualize something, we can imagine all the details about it. Visualizing a goal can help motivate us to achieve it by giving us an idea of how wonderful it will feel to accomplish it. Try this visualization exercise. It might help to close your eyes and have someone else read the steps to you so you can really focus on the picture you are creating in your mind.

1. Calm your body by taking deep breaths and releasing any wiggles or tension.

2. Imagine that you see a mountain.

3. Notice the shape and features of the mountain.

4. Think about a goal you have.

5. Imagine that your goal is at the top of that mountain. How far away is it? How steep is the climb?

6. Start climbing the mountain in your mind.

7. Notice how you feel as you get closer and closer to the top, and closer to your goal.

8. Picture yourself reaching the top.

9. Say out loud to yourself, "I have reached my goal."

10. Notice how you feel.

My Goal Selfie

In the last exercise, you practiced visualizing reaching your goal. In this exercise, you will draw a "selfie" of you reaching your goal.

Think about these questions as you are drawing: What are you doing? What is the expression on your face? How can you show your feelings in the drawing?

What do you need to learn first?

When you set a goal, it can seem difficult and even overwhelming at first. It is helpful to take some time to think about the knowledge and skills you already have that will help you, and then decide what else you need to learn. Many things that seem difficult just involve learning new things.

ASK YOURSELF THESE QUESTIONS:

- What do I already know that will help me achieve this goal?
- What can I already do that will help me achieve this goal?
- What new things do I need to learn to help me achieve this goal?
- What steps can I take to learn these new things?
- What resources can I use to help me learn these new things?
- Who can help me learn these new things?

Answering these questions will help you start setting a clear path to reaching your goal. Setting a clear path to your goal is a great strategy because it can keep you on track and motivated. If you have a goal with no path, it might feel like it's too far away or you have no idea how to get there. Many goals include multiple steps. If you know what steps to take in order to reach your goal, you can see the end more clearly.

There are several strategies you can take to help you break your goal into steps. Take a look at these strategies, and then start planning for your goal!

- Create **milestones**. Milestones are different points along your path that let you know you are getting closer to your goal. For example, if you set a goal to learn all 15 of your spelling words by the end of the week, your milestones could look like this:

  - Milestone 1: Learn to spell words 1 through 5.
  - Milestone 2: Learn to spell words 6 through 10.
  - Milestone 3: Learn to spell words 11 through 15.
  - End Goal: Spell all 15 words correctly.

- Make a list of the tasks you need to achieve. A task is a single action that needs to be completed.

- Create a **timeline**. A timeline shows you when each milestone or task needs to be completed. At the end of your timeline, you will have reached your goal.

Next Time . . .

I set a goal to become a chess player. I didn't know where to start because I had never played before. Eventually, I just gave up because I didn't have a plan. Next time, I will think about what I need to learn and set a path to achieve my goal.

Knowledge Is Power

Think about a goal you would like to achieve. Take time to brainstorm what knowledge you already have that will help you achieve this goal. Next, think about what you still need to learn to reach your goal. Decide what steps you need to take to learn these new things.

Set a goal:

What knowledge do you already have?

What do you still need to learn?

How can you learn it?

Step by Step

When we set goals, trying to figure out where to start can seem overwhelming. Breaking a goal into smaller, shorter steps helps give you a clear path to your goal.

Think of a goal you want to achieve. What is it?

Write one step you can take to get closer to that goal inside each foot.

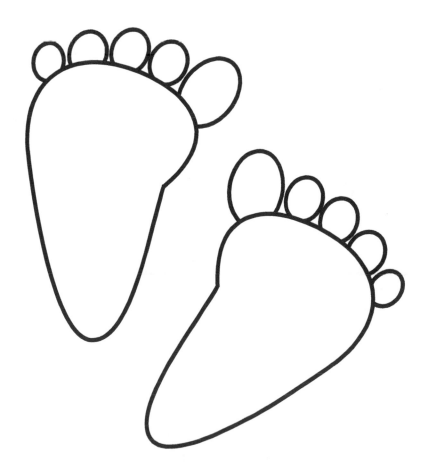

That's Backward!

Backward planning is when you make a plan starting from the end (your goal). You choose the steps from the end to the beginning, working in reverse, to decide how to achieve your goal.

Take a look at this example.

Goal: Sing at the school talent show.

4. Practice performing the song.

3. Come up with dance moves to go with the song.

2. Learn all of the words to the song.

1. Choose a song.

Your turn! Choose a goal you have and come up with a plan using backward planning.

Goal: _____

4. _____

3. _____

2. _____

1. _____

You reached your goal. Now what?

You did it! You made a plan. You followed the path to your goal. You learned new things. You put in all that time and hard work, and you reached your goal. So now what?

First, you should celebrate! You worked so hard! You deserve to soak it all in. Before you even start working toward a goal, you can set a personal reward for when you achieve it. Rewards can include eating your favorite snack, doing your favorite activity, taking some time to relax, or anything else that makes you feel great. Knowing you are working toward a personal reward can help motivate you along the path, as well as give you a fun way to celebrate your success. Take time to celebrate and then start thinking about what's next.

So what *is* next? Just because you reach a goal doesn't mean you have to stop there! You can think about how you can push yourself even further with your current goal. Maybe you learned all your multiplication facts through 10, and now you want to take it a step further and learn 11s and 12s. You can also think about a brand-new goal. What is something else that you want to accomplish? You should always have your next goal in mind. Don't stop thinking about all the great things you can achieve!

HERE ARE SOME QUESTIONS YOU CAN ASK YOURSELF TO HELP YOU BRAINSTORM NEW GOALS:

- What did I learn while reaching my goal that can help me reach another goal?

- What am I prepared to try now?

- What else do I want to learn?

- What else do I want to accomplish?

- What will make me even more proud of myself?

- What is something I have always wanted to do?

- What will make me a better version of myself?

- How can I push myself even further?

- How can I expand on my current goal?

- What small, short-term goals do I need to set in order to reach a big, long-term goal?

In the next exercises, you will practice taking time to reflect on all the amazing things you achieved by reaching a goal, how to take a completed goal to the next level, and how to dream even *bigger* than before.

Mirror, Mirror on the Wall

Think about a goal you have achieved. Imagine you are looking at yourself in a mirror. What do you see that makes you proud? What did you do a great job with while achieving your goal? How did you grow? Write three positive statements about yourself inside the mirror.

Move Your Goalpost

Focus on a goal you have achieved. How could you expand that goal or take it to the next level? Imagine you have been kicking a football into a goal, and you are now an expert. Challenge yourself by moving the goalpost back.

Goal I achieved:

_____

_____

How can I take it to the next level?

_____

_____

_____

_____

_____

_____

_____

Dream Bigger!

What is your biggest dream?

_____

_____

How can you make that dream *even* bigger? What else can you achieve?

_____

_____

_____

Write three steps to make that dream happen:

1. _____

2. _____

3. _____

CHAPTER 6

KEEP GOING!

Wow! You have really come a long way with developing your growth mindset. You've almost made it through this whole book, but the work doesn't end here. Don't stop now! In chapter 6, you will learn all about how to push yourself even further. You will learn how to motivate yourself through the hard work and struggles that come along with your goals. This chapter also teaches you the power of positive thinking. You will explore the importance of seeking help and asking questions as you work through challenges. Finally, you will practice strategies for staying curious and filling your brain with new things. You are ready to learn and practice some tools that will help you continue to achieve your goals long after you've finished this book. So let's keep going!

You can do it!

We all need words of encouragement sometimes. This part of the book is here to remind you that *you* can do hard things. And do you know what's great about doing hard things? Hard things allow you to grow. We know from chapter 1 that doing challenging things causes our brains to change and grow through our neurons making connections, but we can grow in other ways, too. Doing hard things grows our **character**, which is the collection of qualities we have that affect the way we think, feel, and act. Examples of character traits that grow when we do hard things include **perseverance**, **determination**, **confidence**, and courage. All your traits have an opportunity to become stronger when you work through challenges and accomplish difficult tasks or goals.

Even though we know hard things can be good for us, there may still come a time when you feel like you aren't good enough at something or just can't do it. Don't feel bad if you are feeling this way. It's just part of the process. What's important is how you decide to handle these feelings. Instead of giving in to them and walking away from a challenge, pick yourself back up and remember *you can do it*!

HERE ARE SOME THINGS YOU CAN TRY WHEN YOU NEED ENCOURAGEMENT:

- Make a list of all the amazing things you have accomplished and read them back to yourself.

- Spend time with a friend or family member who makes you feel good about yourself. Sometimes we need another person to remind us how strong we are. It's okay to ask for encouragement from others.

- Celebrate your progress. Think about what you have achieved so far. There is nothing stopping you from achieving even more.

- Take a moment to thank your brain. When things are challenging, your brain is growing. Have gratitude!

- Be a friend to yourself. Talk to yourself in the same kind and positive way you would talk to a friend.

- Listen to uplifting and positive music. Research shows that uplifting music can actually give your brain a boost, which might be just what you need to push through a tough time.

The exercises in this section will teach you two more strategies to try when you need some encouragement. Keep these tools in your toolbox for when things get hard!

Dear Me: Don't Give Up!

Everyone feels like giving up sometimes, but with a growth mindset, we can push past the doubt and frustration and keep moving forward. Sometimes it takes a friendly reminder of this when we are feeling like we want to give up. Write a letter to yourself, encouraging yourself not to give up. Come back and read it whenever you feel like quitting.

Dear me,

Sincerely,

Here's Why I Am Awesome

Don't forget: *You* are awesome! Think of all the things that make you an awesome kid. List them here and come back to read them whenever you are feeling down.

I am awesome because:

1. _____

2. _____

3. _____

4. _____

5. _____

6. _____

7. _____

8. _____

9. _____

10. _____

Think positive!

As humans, we are *always* thinking. Close your eyes and think about your favorite things about yourself. Did you hear a little voice in your head saying great things about you? This voice is your self-talk. It's the way you talk to yourself inside your head (or out loud). It is so important to practice using *positive* self-talk, which means we are talking to ourselves in a kind, respectful, and encouraging way.

Not convinced about the power of positive thinking? Take a look at some of these benefits:

- Improves attitude
- Increases confidence
- Promotes self-love
- Helps you cope with stress
- Helps you work through challenges

Having a positive statement that you can go back to and say out loud or in your head can be powerful and helpful. For example, if you have a big test coming up and you know you will be very nervous, a positive saying you could try is this: "I am prepared, and I will do my best." This positive thought will help calm any anxiety about taking the test and will give you the reassurance that you have done everything you can to do your best on the test. You can repeat it to yourself before and during your test to keep yourself feeling positive.

Keeping up with all your positive statements is a great way to look back and give yourself some encouragement when you need it. Here are some things you can do with your positive statements:

- Write them in a notebook and add to the list as you think of more.
- Write them on sticky notes and place them somewhere you will see them when you need the reminder.
- Make a recording of yourself saying them out loud so you can listen when you need some help thinking positively.

Use the following exercises to practice positive self-talk. These are great strategies to get your positive thoughts flowing.

Next Time . . .

I love playing on my school's softball team, but sometimes when I go up to bat, I get really frustrated and upset when I get a strike. I start to talk to myself in a mean way and then I lose my confidence. Sometimes this keeps me from doing my best. Next time I get a strike, I will repeat my positive self-talk statement: "It's okay to mess up. I can still be successful because I keep trying."

Stretch Your Mindset

Try each of these stretches and repeat the positive self-talk statement that goes with it. These exercises will allow you to calm and focus both your mind and your body.

AIRPLANE POSE:

1. Stand on one foot.

2. Lean your body forward.

3. Spread your arms out.

4. Focus on your balance.

Repeat: "I can soar to great heights."

TREE POSE:

1. Begin standing up straight with your feet together and hands at your sides.

2. Bring your palms together at your chest.

3. Bend one knee and bring your foot up.

4. Place your foot flat on your other leg, above or below the knee.

Repeat: "I am strong like a tree."

STAR POSE:

1. Begin standing up straight with your arms at your sides and feet together.

2. Step your feet wide apart.

3. Stretch your arms straight out to the sides.

Repeat: "I am a bright, shining star."

HAPPY BABY POSE:

1. Start by lying flat on your back.

2. Bend your knees in toward your belly.

3. Hold the outsides of your feet.

Repeat: "I am joyful."

BUTTERFLY POSE:

1. Sit on the floor with your back straight.

2. Bring your feet together.

3. Pull your feet toward your body.

4. Drop your knees toward the floor.

Repeat: "I am transforming into a better version of myself."

My Mantra

A **mantra** is a phrase you repeat over and over to help calm or focus your mind. A great example of a mantra is from the book *The Little Engine That Could*, in which the engine repeats, "I think I can, I think I can, I think I can."

Come up with a mantra for yourself and write it on a piece of paper. Place it someplace where you will see it each day. You can write ideas for your mantra on the sticky note on this page.

Never be afraid to ask questions and ask for help

Think about a time when you needed help with something. How did you feel about it? Did you ask someone to help you? Being able to ask for help is actually a very important skill in life. Some people have too much pride to admit they need help, but the truth is, we all need help sometimes, and that's okay! It takes courage to reach out to someone to ask for help, and it is something to be proud of. It can be uncomfortable for some people, but the more you practice, the easier it gets, especially when you have a growth mindset. We learned all about problem solving in chapter 3, and asking for help is just another tool in your problem-solving kit.

An important thing to consider when asking for help is to make sure you have tried a few strategies on your own first. Sometimes a person will ask for help to avoid the hard work that we know is necessary to learn and grow. Once you have worked through some strategies on your own, follow these steps for asking for help:

1. **Decide who can help you.**
2. **Tell them what you are trying to do and what you have already tried.**
3. **Tell them something specific that they can do to help you.**
4. **Thank them for their help.**

Another tool you can add to your problem-solving kit is learning when and how to ask questions. Part of continuing to learn is asking questions. Think about a time in school when you were confused about something and raised your hand to ask about it. What happened? Now think about a time in school when you were confused about something, but you decided *not* to ask a question. What happened then? Most likely, you were more successful when you asked a question. That's because asking questions allows us to clear up our understanding or to learn something new.

Learning how to ask questions the right way can help us get the most helpful information. Here are some tips for asking good questions.

- Know your purpose for asking. Why are you asking the question? What are you hoping to learn?

- Decide who can best help you. Who would know the information you are trying to learn?

- Ask **follow-up questions**. Follow-up questions are related questions that give you more information about the topic.

- Be specific! Let the person know *exactly* what you are trying to learn or understand.

- Most important: Listen carefully to the answer!

Try the following exercises to brainstorm who can help you and to practice forming questions.

Next Time . . .

At the end of our science lesson about plants, my teacher asked if we had any questions. I still didn't understand what photosynthesis was, but I was embarrassed to ask a question, so I didn't raise my hand. She passed out a pop quiz, and the first question was about photosynthesis. I got it wrong. The next time I don't understand something, I will raise my hand and ask a question because I know it will help me learn.

Who Can Help?

Write the name of a person you can go to for help in each of the different areas. Think of someone who has a lot of talent or knowledge in that area.

MATH	
SPORTS	
PROBLEMS WITH A FRIEND	
FINE ARTS (MUSIC, ART, DANCE, DRAMA)	
SCIENCE	
READING AND WRITING	
POSITIVE THINKING OR ENCOURAGEMENT	

Check Out My Questions

Begin a checklist of questions that you would like to find the answers to. Come back to the lines in the book to write down new questions any time you think of something else you want to learn about. Whenever you get a question answered, place a check in the box next to it.

❑ --

❑ --

❑ --

❑ --

❑ --

❑ --

❑ --

❑ --

❑ --

❑ --

❑ --

❑ --

Stay curious

We never run out of things to learn. There are always new ideas to explore, new places to see, and new things to try. When you stay curious, you give your brain so many opportunities to grow and change.

SOME WAYS TO BE MORE CURIOUS:

Read more books. Reading is a great way to soak up more knowledge. You can learn about real-life events and people through nonfiction books or explore valuable lessons through characters in fiction books. Many of the most successful people in the world have said that they spend time reading every single day.

Pay attention to people around you. Notice how others act. Talk to people about their experiences. We all have a lot to learn from each other!

Research things. With technology, we have so much information at our fingertips. Ask a parent or teacher to help you use these tools to research things you are curious about.

Don't be afraid to look silly. People often hold themselves back from having new experiences or learning new things because they are afraid of looking silly or failing in front of others. Don't let this hold you back! Most people will respect you just for trying.

Do things you have never done before. Take an art class, learn a new language, or try a new sport. Doing things that are unfamiliar to us is a great way to spark those connections between the neurons in our brains.

Experiment. Experimenting is a great way to use your curiosity to learn something new. Ask a teacher or parent for some safe science experiment ideas that you can try.

Allow your mind to wander and notice where it takes you. Our minds are often curious, even when we aren't trying to be! Pay attention to your thoughts. You can even write them down and explore them further later.

Pay attention to what's around you. Instead of paying attention to a phone, tablet, or other device, notice what's really going on around you. Be curious about your surroundings.

Go to museums, zoos, and aquariums. These are all great places to learn something new and spark your curiosity about a new topic.

Don't stop thinking like a kid! Kids have a natural curiosity because they have so many new things to learn and such great imaginations. Keep it up!

The next two exercises will help you practice using your curiosity.

Fill My Brain

There are so many things to learn! Brainstorm all the things you are curious to learn more about and write them inside the brain.

3, 2, Wonder

Choose a topic or question that you are curious about. Do some research! You can use the internet, look in some books, or ask someone questions.

Write three things you learned:

1. _____

2. _____

3. _____

Write two interesting facts:

1. _____

2. _____

Write one question you still have about this topic.

1. _____

Look How Far You've Come!

You have worked so hard on your growth mindset throughout this book. Let's see how much you've grown! Answer each question with honesty. Remember that part of having a growth mindset is being honest with yourself about your areas of growth. We don't need to be perfect!

EVENT	I WOULD . . .	OR I WOULD . . .
You have tried over and over to build the model airplane, but you just can't figure it out.	Put it away because I'm not smart enough to do it.	Ask for help from someone I know is great at building model airplanes.
Your teacher told you that the reason you are behind on your math work is because you have spent your time talking.	Ignore what she says. She just doesn't like me. She always wants me to be in trouble.	Think about her feedback. She wants me to be successful, and I really do spend a lot of time talking to friends.
You set a goal to raise $100 for your school fundraiser. It's harder than you thought it was going to be.	Give up on the goal. It was just too much money.	Brainstorm new ideas for raising money in the community.
You tried out for the school play. You didn't get the main part that you wanted, but you got a smaller part.	Quit the play. I only want the main role. A smaller role is a waste of my time.	Use the opportunity to practice for next year. I can learn a lot from any role.
You worked really hard studying for your science test, but you still got a low grade.	Stop studying for science. I'll just never be good at it. It's not my thing.	Talk to my teacher about how I am struggling. Maybe he has some suggestions that I could try.

Exercise *continued*

EVENT	I WOULD . . .	OR I WOULD . . .
You met your speed goal on the swim team at practice.	Awesome! I did it! I can stop practicing.	I'm proud of myself. I wonder how much further I can push myself.
You submitted a poem to the school poetry contest. You got third place.	Stop writing poems because I wanted to be in first place.	Keep writing. Third place is great, and if I keep practicing, I might get first place next year.
You are learning a new skill in math. The rest of the class seems to get it, but you are still very confused.	Say, "I just can't do this kind of math."	Say, "I just can't do this kind of math, *yet.*"
Your friends told you they don't like playing games with you when you always have to be the one to go first.	Stop playing with those friends. They are just being mean, and I can find someone else to play with.	Reflect on what they said. How would I feel if someone else always wanted to go first? I'll apologize and take turns.
Your teacher gives out a reward for good behavior each week. You've never gotten it.	Stop trying so hard to get it. Who cares about a behavior reward anyway?	Keep up the good behavior. It will help me in other ways, even if I don't earn the reward.

Count the number of purple answers you chose. This will be your growth mindset score. _____ /10

Go back to the quiz you took in chapter 1 and see how much you have grown!

Believe in yourself . . . and put in the work

You have come so far! Take some time to celebrate the hard work you have done by going through each of the exercises in this book. You chose to become a better version of yourself by learning all about a growth mindset.

Let's take a look back at some of the things you have learned through this book. Read each statement out loud and then pat yourself on the back as you say, "I'm proud of me!"

"I have learned about the difference between a growth mindset and a fixed mindset. I understand the power of 'yet' and can use it to help me have a growth mindset. I'm proud of me!"

"I understand how AWESOME mistakes are. I can look at my mistakes as an opportunity to learn and grow. I can also recognize and manage my emotions when I make mistakes that leave me feeling frustrated. I'm proud of me!"

"I learned strategies for problem solving. Now I understand how challenges help my brain grow. I also understand how feedback is meant to help me learn and grow, so I can use feedback to help me. I'm proud of me!"

"I practiced using creative thinking. I can think outside the box and use my creative brain when I am stuck on a challenge. I'm proud of me!"

"I can set goals and create a path to achieving them. I understand that some-times goals require learning new things or asking questions. I am ready to achieve my goals. I am proud of me!"

"I can use positive thinking to help me be successful. I am a curious learner, and I know how to ask questions and ask for help. I am proud of me!"

Wow! Look at all the new skills you have. You are AMAZING!

A growth mindset is something we are *always* working on. A growth mindset is like a superpower to battle negative habits and thinking. You might still sometimes catch yourself thinking with a fixed mindset or practicing negative self-talk. These tendencies are normal. Don't be too hard on yourself. What's important is that you notice when it happens and use this growth mindset superpower to change your thinking and your attitude.

Working on our mindset never ends, but as we've learned from this book, hard work means our brains are growing. So keep it up! And when things get challenging or frustrating, come back here for the brain boost you need to push through.

GLOSSARY

accountable: responsible for something and expected to get it done

affirmation: something we say to ourselves to offer encouragement and self-love

brainstorming: thinking hard to generate ideas about something

character: qualities that shape the way someone thinks, feels, and behaves

confidence: a belief or feeling that you can be successful

consequence: something that happens as a result of a decision or an action

creativity: the ability to make new things or have new ideas

curiosity: the desire to learn or know more

determination: a quality that causes someone to work toward achieving something even if it's difficult

feedback: information received from someone to help us improve

fixed mindset: the belief that our abilities, talents, and intelligence are static

follow-up questions: related questions that provide more information about a topic

goal: a desire that is put into action by way of a plan; something you are trying to complete or achieve

growth mindset: the belief that our abilities, talents, and intelligence can grow or change through effort and perseverance

long-term goals: goals that take years of planning and action

long-term solution: a lasting resolution to a problem

mantra: a word or phrase to repeat to help focus on a belief

milestones: important points in the progress toward a goal

mindfulness: being aware of the present moment

mistake: an action or choice that is wrong or incorrect

neurons: tiny cells in the brain that transmit and receive nerve impulses to send messages throughout the body

perseverance: pushing through challenges even when it feels impossible

problem solving: the process of finding a solution to a problem, usually through a variety of strategies

reflecting: thinking deeply about something

self-talk: talking to the self out loud or in the mind

short-term goals: goals that take days or months of planning and action

timeline: a schedule displaying a planned order or sequence

visualization: the ability to create pictures in the mind

RESOURCES FOR KIDS

To check out any of these resources, ask a grown-up to go to Thesocialemotionalteacher.com/growthmindset to find the links.

BOOKS

After the Fall: How Humpty Dumpty Got Back Up Again by Dan Santat

You've probably heard the story of Humpty Dumpty and his great fall, but what happened after? Learn how Humpty Dumpty used a growth mindset to get back up again.

Beautiful Oops! by Barney Saltzberg

Here is a cheerful look at just how awesome our mistakes are, because sometimes they can be an opportunity to make something beautiful.

Your Fantastic Elastic Brain: Stretch It, Shape It by JoAnn Deak, PhD

This will teach you all about how you can stretch and shape your brain through a growth mindset. Learn how your brain is like a muscle and how mistakes make it stronger.

WEBSITES

PBS Kids Problem-Solving Games

Explore tons of fun games to help you practice problem solving! Ask a grownup to help you access the website (pbskids.org/games/problem-solving) to get started.

PODCASTS

The Big Life Kids Podcast

This will help you develop a growth mindset through engaging stories about Leo and Zara, two silly best friends who are on a mission to discover real-life growth mindset stories.

Wow in the World

This is perfect for expanding your curiosity and learning new things! The hosts, Mindy and Guy, will guide you on a journey to discover cool stories in science and technology. This is a great podcast to listen to with the whole family.

RESOURCES FOR GROWN-UPS

For links to any of these resources, go to
Thesocialemotionalteacher.com/growthmindset.

BOOKS

How Children Succeed by Paul Tough

This discusses the importance of a child's character (skills like perseverance, self-esteem, optimism, and curiosity) being the key factor to their success.

Mindset: The New Psychology of Success by Carol S. Dweck

Carol Dweck explores the psychology behind growth mindset and discusses how we can learn to fulfill our potential in relation to business, parenting, school, and relationships.

Mindsets for Parents: Strategies to Encourage Growth Mindsets in Kids by Mary Cay Ricci and Margaret Lee

Written by two educational consultants, this book gives parents tips for increasing effort, perseverance, and hard work in kids. It is designed to provide a road map for developing a home environment in which the growth mindset thrives.

ARTICLES

"Fixed vs. Growth: The Two Basic Mindsets That Shape Our Lives" by Maria Popova

This article breaks down the difference between a fixed mindset and a growth mindset and describes the impact each one can have on our lives.

"10 Phrases to Help You Develop a Growth Mindset in Parenting" by Alissa Zorn

This provides parents with strategies through ten simple phrases to develop a growth mindset of their own in their role as parents.

WEBSITES

BigLifeJournal.com

This is a great place to go for products you can use with your child at home to continue developing a growth mindset. Be sure to check out the blog for great articles covering many aspects of a growth mindset.

MindsetKit.org

This site is full of helpful resources for parents. It explores what a growth mindset is, why it's important, and the best practices for the development of a growth mindset in the home. Includes resource sections for mentors and educators.

PODCASTS

The Balanced Educator, Episode 99: Mindfulness & Growth Mindset with Teacher Jenelle Gagné

This episode is a discussion about growth mindset with teacher and mom Jenelle Gagné. She provides insight and strategies for implementing a growth mindset in the classroom or at home.

Sunshine Parenting, Episode 5: Using a Growth Mindset with Jeff Cheley

In this episode, Jeff Cheley describes his experiences with growth mindset as a summer camp director and father of three.

INDEX

A

Accidental Success learning opportunities, 29
Accountability, 90, 130
ADHD, 15
Advice for a Friend exercise, 48
Affirmations, 40, 130
All Shapes and Sizes exercise, 24–25
A-*Maze*-ing Improvement exercise, 55
Asking for help, 117–120
    asking questions, 117–118, 120
    exercises, 119–120
Asking questions, 117–118, 120

B

Backward planning, 100
Belly breaths, 39
Better Today exercise, 54
Brain
    ability to change, ix, 1, 11
    encouragement for, 12, 13
    and improving, 53
    neurons in, 10–11
Brainstorming
    and curiosity, 123
    defined, 130
    new goals, 84, 102, 104–105
Break It Down exercise, 80–81
Breaks, taking, 38

C

Celebrating, 127
    and challenges, 57
    and encouragement, 109
    and improving, 53
    and reaching goals, 101, 103
Challenges, 56–60. *See also* Trying new things
    and brain, 11, 53
    and character, 108
    exercises, 58–60
    tips for, 56–57
Character, 108, 130
Check Out My Questions exercise, 120
Chocolate chip cookies, 34

Confidence, 108, 130
Consequences, 22–23, 24–25, 130
Courage, 108
Creativity, 68–72
    defined, 68–69, 130
    exercises, 70–72
    and frustration, 38
    and no limits, 84
    tips for, 69
Curiosity, ix, 121–124
    and creativity, 69
    paths to, 121–122
Cyrus, Miley, 36

D

Dear Me: Don't Give Up! exercise, 110
Dear Mistake exercise, 37
Deep breaths, 19
Determination, 108, 130
Drawing in the Dark exercise, 20–21
Draw Outside the Box exercise, 70
Dream Bigger! exercise, 105
Dyslexia, 14

E

Edison, Thomas, 35, 86
Einstein, Albert, 36
Emotions. *See* Feelings
Encouragement
    for brain, 12, 13
    and challenges, 57
    and character, 108
    exercises, 110–111
    and frustration, 39
    and self-talk, 7
    tips for, 109
Exercises
    asking for help, 119–120
    challenges, 58–60
    creativity, 70–72
    encouragement, 110–111
    feedback, 51–52
    frustration, 40–41

Exercises *(continued)*
    goals, 92, 94–95
    improving, 54–55
    learning opportunities, 31–32, 35, 37
    mistakes, 20–21, 24–26, 31–32, 35–37
    no limits, 85–87
    planning, 79–83
    positive self-talk, 114–116
    practicing, 75–76
    problem solving, 46–48
    "yet," 63–65
Exercising, 38
Experimenting, 122

F

Feedback, 49–52
    defined, 49, 130
    exercises, 51–52
    tips for, 50
Feedback Mindset exercise, 51
Feelings
    and feedback, 49, 50
    managing, ix, 18, 19
    and mistakes, 18–19
Fill My Brain exercise, 123
5-4-3-2-1 practice, 39
Fixed mindset
    and brain, 11
    defined, viii, 2, 130
    feedback exercise, 51
    quizzes, 4–5, 8–9
Flip the Slip exercise, 32
Focus, 90
Follow-up questions, 118, 130
Ford, Henry, 65
Frustration, 38–41
    exercises, 40–41
    and mistakes, 38–39

G

Goals, 90–92
    brainstorming new, 84, 102, 104–105
    celebrating, 101, 103
    defined, 89, 130
    exercises, 92, 94–95

    importance of, 90
    knowledge review for, 96, 98
    long-term and short-term, 90–91, 130, 131
    milestones for, 97, 99
    planning for, 96–100
    reaching, 101, 103
    and visualization, 93–95
"Good/bad" labels, 56
Gratitude, 13
Grown-ups, information for, viii–ix, 133–134
Growth mindset
    defined, viii, 1, 3, 130
    examples of, 14–15
    feedback exercise, 51
    and mistakes, 18
    modeling, ix
    quizzes, 4–5, 8–9
    self-evaluation, 125–126
    tips for, 6

H

Here's Why I Am Awesome exercise, 111

I

I Can See It Now . . . exercise, 94
If I Never Made a Mistake . . . exercise, 35
I Knew Better learning opportunities, 29
Imagination, 69
Improving, 53–55
    and brain, 53
    and definition of growth mindset, 3
    exercises, 54–55
    and feedback, 49
    and goals, 90
    and learning opportunities, 23
    and perseverance, 53
    "yet," 61–65

J

Jordan, Michael, 87
Just Like the Movies exercise, 59

K

Keep On Rolling exercise, 41
Knowledge Is Power exercise, 98

L

Learning opportunities, 28–31
    exercises, 31–32, 35, 37
    types of, 29–30
Learning styles, 56
Learning to Love It exercise, 60
Lee, Bruce, 36
Let's Do It Again . . . and Again exercise, 75
Limiting thoughts, 84–87
The Little Engine That Could, 116
Long-term goals, 90–91, 130
Long-term solutions, 78, 82–83, 131
Look How I've Grown! exercise, 54

M

Mantras, 116, 131
Mazes, 55
Milestones, 97, 99, 131
Mindfulness, 39, 131
Mirror, Mirror on the Wall exercise, 103
Mistakes
    accepting, ix
    accepting responsibility for, 27
    awesome results of, 34
    and brain, 13
    choices about, 19
    consequences of, 22–23, 24–25
    defined, 131
    exercises, 20–21, 24–26, 31–32, 35–37
    and feelings, 18–19
    and frustration, 38–39
    learning from, 17, 28–32, 35, 37
    quotes about, 35–36
    reflecting on, 22–23
    your plan for, 33
More Than a Band-Aid exercise, 82–83
More Than One Solution exercise, 47
Motivation, 56, 90
Move Your Goalpost exercise, 104
Multiple solutions, 47, 69
Music
    and encouragement, 109
    and frustration, 38
My Goal Selfie exercise, 95
My Mantra exercise, 116
My Problem Plan exercise, 46

N

Neurons, 10 11, 53, 131
Never Again learning opportunities, 30
New things. *See* Trying new things
No limits, 84–87
    exercises, 85–87

O

One Step Closer learning opportunities, 29
"Oops" Feeling exercise, 20
Open mind, 69

P

Perseverance
    and character, 108
    and frustration, 38
    and goals, 131
    and improving, 53
    and self-talk, 11
Planning, 77–83
    backward, 100
    backward planning, 100
    exercises, 79–83
    knowledge review, 96, 98
    and milestones, 97, 99
Playing, 69
Positive Affirmations exercise, 40
Positive self-talk, 112–116
    benefits of, 112
    exercises, 114–116
Practicing, 73–76
    and definition of growth mindset, 3
    exercises, 75–76
    importance of, 73
    strategies for, 74
Praise, ix, 13. *See also* Encouragement
Pretending, 69
Problem solving, 44–48
    and asking questions, 117–118
    blocks to, 45
    and creativity, 38
    defined, 44, 131
    exercises, 46–48
    understanding the problem, 44

Q

Questions, 117–118, 120

R

Reading, 121
Reflecting
    defined, 131
    on mistakes, 22–23
    for planning, 79
Research, 121, 124
Resources, 132–134
Responsibility, 27
Ross, Bob, 36
Rowling, J. K., 86

S

Saint-Exupéry, Antoine de, 77
Saying Is Believing exercise, 85
Say What? exercise, 35
Self-talk
    and brain, 11–12
    defined, 131
    and encouragement, 7
    exercises, 85
    positive, 112–116
    and problem solving, 45
    "yet," 61–65
Short-term goals, 90–91, 131
Silly Putty, 34
Silly Solutions exercise, 72
Snacks, 38
Sports, 14, 15
Step by Step exercise, 99
Stretch Your Mindset exercise, 114–115

T

Things I Can't Do . . . Yet exercise, 63
Think, Restate, Thank, Decide exercise, 52

Think Before You Plan exercise, 79
Thinking. *See* Reflecting
This Used to Be a . . . exercise, 71
3, 2, Wonder exercise, 124
Timelines, 97
To My Friend Who Doesn't Practice exercise, 76
Trying new things
    and brain, 11
    and creativity, 69
    and curiosity, 121
    and definition of growth mindset, 3
    and improving, 53
    and mistakes, 34, 36

U

Use What You've Got exercise, 64

V

Visualization, 93–95, 131

W

Wakefield, Ruth, 34
What Challenges Me? exercise, 58–59
What If They Had Given Up? exercise, 86–87
What Went Wrong exercise, 26
Wheel of Fortune exercise, 92
Who Can Help? exercise, 119
A World Without Goals exercise, 92
Wright, James, 34

Y

"Yet," 61–65
    exercises, 63–65
You're Right exercise, 65
You're the Expert exercise, 31

ACKNOWLEDGMENTS

I wouldn't be writing this book if it weren't for the passion that has been lit inside my heart by every student I have ever taught. Thank you for allowing me to learn the power of the growth mindset and social emotional learning right along with you. There is nothing more beautiful than the heart of a child, and I love each of you dearly. You have made me better.

I would like to thank my parents, John and Shannon Curley, for being the first to instill a growth mindset in me. A large part of a growth mindset revolves around providing children with a safe space to make mistakes and grow from them. I am fortunate to have grown up in a home where I never questioned my worth or their love for me, regardless of the mistakes I made. I love you, Mom and Dad.

I can't end this book without a shout-out to my support system: Steve Hehir (and the entire Hehir family), Buck Curley, Lindsey Breeding, Kristen Bright, Whitney Wagner, Brittany Walker, and Amanda Thompson, who cheered me on every step of the way as I wrote my first book. My love and gratitude for each of you is immeasurable.

Finally, thank you to Callisto Media and my amazing editor, Samantha Barbaro, for allowing me this incredible opportunity to share my passion for growth mindset with children through this book.

ABOUT THE AUTHOR

Peyton Curley is a former teacher who used her experience and passion for working with children to start her business, The Social Emotional Teacher, LLC. She is devoted to providing parents, educators, and mental health workers with the resources and strategies they need to develop and nurture social emotional learning skills in children. She has seen the power of social emotional learning firsthand through her work as an educator, and wants to empower students of all backgrounds through SEL.

Peyton lives in St. Petersburg, Florida, where she enjoys spending time with her dogs, Crouton and Poptart, reading books, watching Kentucky basketball, and soaking up the warm weather.

Printed in the USA
CPSIA information can be obtained
at www.ICGtesting.com
CBHW041608030424
6190CB00002B/3